THE CADOGANS
AT WAR

THE
CADOGANS
AT WAR
1783–1864

*The Third Earl Cadogan
and His Family*

ROBERT PEARMAN

Haggerston Press

LONDON

For John

Frontispiece:
George, 3rd Earl Cadogan
by Sir Francis Grant

First published 1990
by the Haggerston Press
38 Kensington Place, London w8 7PR

Typeset by Fakenham Photosetting Ltd,
Fakenham, Norfolk
Printed in Great Britain
by Redwood Press Ltd, Melksham

1 869812 05 0

Contents

Do well the duty
that lies before you

Pittacus, c. 675 BC

Foreword

As a near life-long devotee of C.S. Forester's sea-going hero Horatio Hornblower, my interest in George Cadogan was immediately engaged when, researching an earlier book, *The Cadogan Estate*, I discovered that his first ship as a twelve-year-old First Class Volunteer was H.M. frigate *Indefatigable*, refitting at Plymouth in December 1795 and commanded by Captain Sir Edward Pellew. For this was the vessel on which the young Hornblower notionally served from the spring of 1794 until 1797 when he was captured by the Spanish. In my mind's eye, when George first went below to the midshipmen's berth the tall, gawky figure of Hornblower was there to give him a sympathetic welcome: fact meeting fiction. I knew intimately the fictional sailor's subsequent glittering career, and of his marriage to the imaginary Lady Barbara Wellesley, but what of his flesh-and-blood contemporary? In the event, I found that George's time afloat had all the ingredients of a recent Royal Navy officer recruitment advertisement – 'Challenge – Excitement – Responsibility – Variety – Travel – Promotion'.[1] After initial service in the French Revolutionary Wars he was actively employed during the ensuing Napoleonic and Peninsular Wars until December 1813 when, as a post captain, he went ashore for the last time having survived much shot, shell, tempest, mutiny, and capture by the French.

In George's family circumstances, I struck a rich vein of social drama and entanglement. As a younger son, there seemed little chance of George inheriting the family titles and estates as two half-brothers and an elder brother, Henry, had prior claims. They were all, however, destined to die without a legal heir between them; Henry, on the battlefield at Vittoria. Four other half-brothers had died before George was born; three in the service of their country. Two of his sisters,

[7]

Lady Emily and Lady Charlotte, married brothers of the future Duke of Wellington with disastrous results for these particular real-life Wellesleys. To protect the family honour George fought a duel with the 'greatest cavalry leader of the day'[2] on Wimbledon Common.

Unlike his distant cousin Nelson, George did not achieve flag rank until late in life, by the process of slowly ascending the Navy list. He was one of that band of dedicated captains who remained at sea in harsh and often dangerous conditions, year after year, to protect and to advance the British cause. For his pains, he has been described as 'pitiless'[3] and 'inhumane'[4] due to his use of the lash; which raises the question as to whether there was any alternative means of enforcing discipline.

A study of the 3rd Earl Cadogan and his family presents an absorbing insight into English society during one of it's liveliest periods.

BATH   *Robert Pearman*
September 1989

[8]

CHAPTER I

The Family

The Honourable George Cadogan was born on Monday the 5th May 1783 at 14, St James's Square, a second son for the 3rd Baron Cadogan of Oakley, Bucks, by his second wife, the former Mary Churchill. Although the sun shone brightly there was still a keen edge to the day and fires crackled in the grates of the five-storey house, tucked away in the north-west corner of the first of the West End squares. The houses forming the quadrangle, conveniently placed for access to both St James's Palace and Parliament, had been built in the 1670s on the initiative of Lord St Albans, and their occupants represented a microcosm of the tight-knit English aristocracy, including the Dukes of Norfolk and Leeds and the Earls of Bristol, Dartmouth and Strafford. Their main rooms overlooked the central garden square laid to lawn, and the generally peaceful air was disturbed only by the occasional rattle and rumble of horse-drawn carriages passing over the cobbled roadway. The Cadogan's house was simply built with sash

St James's Square, west side, in the 18th century

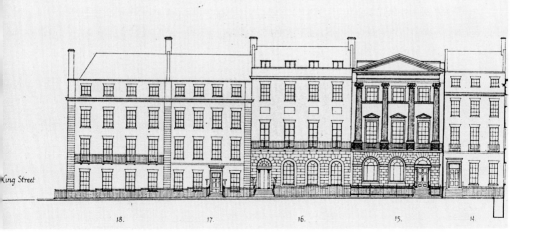

King Street

18.   17.   16.   15.   14.

Anne Oldfield

windows under a slate roof and if the bricks were originally
pink, the colour would have long since disappeared under a
layer of London soot. There was a front area with iron rail-
ings, and stone steps led to a panelled front door. Architectur-
ally, it was 'the worst house in the Square'[1]; certainly it had
the smallest frontage.

In the main bedroom on the second floor, Lady Cadogan
was cared for by her maid and confidante, the unusually
named Mrs Farley Murray Bull. Lady Cadogan, a great-great
niece of John Churchill, the 1st Duke of Marlborough, had

recently celebrated her thirty-third birthday and now that George, her fourth child, had safely arrived, she could give full attention to the pleasures of the London season that had just begun and would last until the end of July, providing for the fashionable élite a constant round of balls, theatres and parties. George, meantime, would be placed in the care of a wet-nurse. Lady Cadogan was the younger of two daughters born to Colonel Charles and Lady Mary Churchill, who shared their time between homes in London and Nancy, the historic capital of Lorraine in north-east France. Colonel Churchill was the illegitimate or natural son of General Charles Churchill and Anne Oldfield, an actress whose 'personal graces won recognition rather than her abilities'.[2] General Churchill, who died in 1745, in turn was the natural child of another General Charles Churchill,. brother of the 1st Duke of Marlborough, by a lady whose identity is unrecorded; Anne Oldfield died in 1730 and was buried in Westminster Abbey. Lady Cadogan's mother, Lady Mary Churchill, was yet another natural child whose mother, the 'vivacious' Maria Skerrett, was a mistress of Sir Robert Walpole, generally regarded as the first Prime Minister. For

Sir Robert Walpole   *Maria Skerrett*

many years he 'had managed the nation's affairs with consummate skill and ability.' The parents married following the death of Sir Robert's first wife and their daughter, on her father's advancement to the earldom of Orford in 1742, was granted a patent of precedence as an Earl's daughter by George II. Lord Orford's youngest son from his first marriage was Horace Walpole, the author and letter-writer, and his greatnephew, Horatio Walpole, was married to Lady Cadogan's sister, Sophia. Before her marriage to Lord Cadogan in 1777, at the comparatively late age of 27, Mary Churchill had lived life to the full in both French and English society. 'On la trouve jolie, et qu'elle ressemble en beau à notre Dauphine [Marie Antoinette].' ' . . . la Maréchale de Mirepoix l'aime à la folie. Elle a eu la meilleure education du monde; elle est attentive, obligeante, elle a de la gaîté, de la grâce.'[3] It would be surprising if, therefore, Lady Cadogan was anything other than intelligent, resolute and sensual.

Lord Cadogan, whose coat of arms bore the motto 'Qui Invidet Minor Est'[4], was in his fifty-fifth year and if his house in St James's Square was a little cramped he would not have worried overmuch for he had other, more spacious residences in London. His Lordship of the Manor of Chelsea, arising from a moiety interest, was administered from Cadogan House, which lay off the Kings Road, while his political life as an active member of the House of Lords centred upon Cadogan House in Whitehall, with other houses in nearby Scotland Yard and St Albans Street. Away from the demands of the capital, Lord Cadogan took his ease at Caversham Lodge, the family seat in Oxfordshire, with occasional visits to his more recently acquired estate at Santon Downham, straddling the Norfolk–Suffolk border. Charles Sloane Cadogan, an only child, succeeded to the barony in 1776 on the death of his father, Charles Cadogan, who had inherited the title from his elder brother, the 1st Earl Cadogan, upon whose death in 1726 the earldom lapsed in the absence of a direct male heir; the barony survived due to a special remainder. Charles matricu-

Mrs Charles Cadogan
(née Frances Bromley)

Charles, 3rd Baron
Cadogan of Oakley

lated at Magdalen College, Oxford, in 1746 and in May of the following year, at the age of 18, he married Frances Bromley, daughter of Lord Montfort, a former Whig Member of Parliament for Cambridge. Opting then for a political career, Charles was duly elected in his turn for the university city from 1749–76, with one short break in 1754–5 when the seat was represented by his brother-in-law Thomas Bromley.

The Cadogan family's politics were solidly Whig, stemming more particularly from the 1st Earl's involvement with the 1st Duke of Marlborough and the accession of the Hanoverian dynasty in 1714. Charles and Frances had seven children. In 1749 an heir, Charles Henry, was born followed by William (1751), Thomas (1752), and George in 1754. A daughter, Mary, was born in 1756 and two years later came Edward followed finally by Henry who died in 1774 having just entered his teens. The family lived at Caversham together with Charles's father and his mother Elizabeth, the younger daughter of the late Sir Hans Sloane, and all appears to have gone well until early in 1755 when Lord Montfort, in dire financial straits, committed suicide. 'His strange end surprised me a good deal, as he seemed as happy as a great taste for pleasure, and an ample fortune to gratify it could make him', wrote Lady Hervey to a friend afterwards, going on to describe the extreme deliberation with which his lordship read over his will three times with his lawyer, sealed it up, and shot himself through the head before the man had got downstairs.[5]

The death of her father was a severe shock for Frances, compounded by the loss of her only daughter, Mary, fourteen months later. Perhaps she never fully recovered her balance from these unhappy events and when her mother-in-law Lady Cadogan died suddenly on the 20th May 1768, Frances went into an immediate decline and died before the week was out; both were buried in the family vault in St Peter's, Caversham. Lady Mary Coke visited the Lodge two months later and wrote 'I inquired of the Maid who shew'd us the House what occasion'd her death, and She told me it was intirely owing to the shock of Her Mother in law's death, that she was never well from that moment, and went quite distracted. At the end of four days she dyed raving mad.' The diarist had earlier confided that Lady Cadogan had 'left the interest of four score thousand that She had in her power to Lord Cadogan for his life, then to her Son, and intailed it upon her Grandson.'[6]

In the year following his wife's death, Charles Cadogan was appointed to the lucrative office of Master of the Mint and the ever-watchful Horace Walpole recorded that, 'in 1774 when the light guineas were called in and recoined, he was computed to have made £30,000 by his profit on the recoinage'.[7] To Mary Churchill, he must have appeared an eminently well qualified suitor; for him it was an opportunity, in his middle years, for a fresh start. The marriage settlement was signed on the 6th August 1777, providing for the sum of £25,000 to be invested in 'lands and Tenements' for Mary's eventual benefit and, this formality over, the ceremony took place at St Peter's two days later, witnessed by Mary's father and William Cadogan, now a cleric and rector of St Lukes, Chelsea. Of the occasion, Horace Walpole wrote, 'My niece's match with Lord Cadogan, since she herself approves it, gives me great satisfaction. She is one of the best and most discreet young women in the world, and her husband, I am sure, is fortunate.'[8] Their first child, Emily, was born in the succeeding year, followed by Henry in 1780 and Charlotte in 1781. George was the next to arrive.

There had been three deaths among Lord Cadogan's older children. The War of American Independence, which began in 1775, had claimed the lives of Thomas and Edward, while George had been killed in India in the service of the East India Company. Thomas, a post captain in the Royal Navy, was lost when his ship, the 74-gun *Glorieux*, foundered with the loss of all hands, in an Atlantic gale off Newfoundland in September 1782. Edward, a captain in the 49th Foot, died of yellow fever on St. Lucia in the West Indies in April 1779 after his regiment had fought successfully against the French. All three, seemingly, were bachelors and they died without issue.[9] The eldest son Charles, another bachelor, was commissioned into the 3rd Foot Guards in 1762 and in 1778 he became a captain in the 61st Foot. His name disappears from the army list in 1780 and, in the light of subsequent events, it is likely that he sold out his commission due to ill-health. William had married an army officer's widow from Chelsea, Mrs Jane Bradshaw, in 1782 and in addition to his pastoral duties at Chelsea, he was also vicar of St Giles at Reading, where he lived in preference to his London rectory.

The baby George thrived and as the London season drew to a close he was taken back to Caversham Lodge, to join his brother and sisters. The Mansion house stood on a rise overlooking the Thames, set in a thousand acres of parkland which in 1764 had been landscaped for Lord Cadogan's father by Lancelot 'Capability' Brown. A neighbour writing in 1776 records that 'he (Brown) has made it one of the finest parks imaginable, and at the time of the Whitethorns being in blow, which at Caversham are by far the oldest and most beautiful I

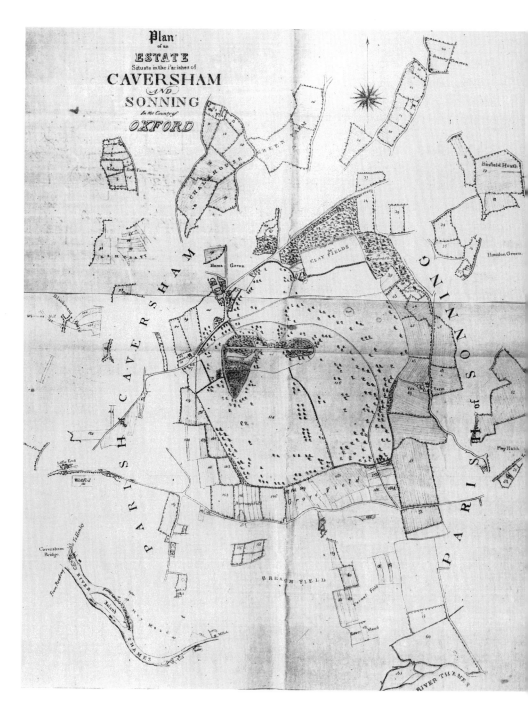

Caversham Lodge Estate

ever saw, 'tis hardly possible to describe the scene it offers. The terrace at Caversham (next to Lord Lincoln's), I've heard is the finest in England.' The ground floor rooms included a 'very elegant library, which you go through to a breakfast-room adjoining the salon, in both of which are many good pictures, but the drawing room beyond the saloon is one of the most pleasing apartments I ever saw, being fitted up with the English tapestry, which in most people's judgement exceeds the Gobelin.... From this room you go through a pretty lobby into the eating room, a very good one.'[10] The first and second floors provided twenty more rooms for use by the family and guests, while the top floor accommodated the servants, presided over by the house steward and butler, Joseph Pearce, and the cook and housekeeper, Mrs Vaughan. Lord Cadogan's immediate needs were looked after by his personal servant, William Lloyd, whilst Mrs Bull continued to care for Lady Cadogan.

The War of American Independence, during which both France (hoping to avenge her defeat in the Seven Years War of 1756–63) and Spain had allied themselves to the colonists, was brought to an end on the 3rd September 1783 by the Treaty of Versailles, whereby great Britain recognised American independence. The war had virtually ended in October 1781, with the surrender at Yorktown of 7000 British troops under Lord Cornwallis, hemmed in by American and French forces and cut off from reinforcement or evacuation by French control of the Atlantic seaboard. This event was a severe blow to the Tory administration of Lord North who, under mounting criticism, resigned as Prime Minister in March 1782. George III, then formed a new administration under Lord Rockingham who appointed a fellow Whig, 'the eloquent and charming, yet fundamentally irresponsible' Charles James Fox as Foreign Secretary. Fox and Lord Cadogan were second cousins, having a common ancestor in the 1st Earl Cadogan whose eldest daughter, Lady Sarah, the Duchess of Richmond, was Fox's maternal grandmother. Lord Rockingham died in July 1782 and was replaced by another Whig, Lord Shelburne, who like Lord Cadogan was a great-grandson of Sir Hardress Waller, a signatory of the death warrant of Charles I. The new Prime Minister dismissed Fox and invited William Pitt, a Tory and younger son of a former premier Lord Chatham, into his Cabinet as Chancellor of the Exchequer, but his ministry was short-lived and he resigned in February 1783.

Fox and his supporters were opposed to Lord Shelburne and had argued that he ought not to have taken office, but instead should have forced the King to allow the House of Commons to choose the Prime Minister. The resignation of Lord Shelburne left the way open for one of a number of possible coalitions; Pitt and Fox might, for example, have come together supporting a policy of reform. In the event, however, Fox made a coalition with Lord North, partly to keep Pitt from power and partly to take revenge on Lord Shelburne. They agreed to serve under the Duke of Portland, a Tory, who became Prime Minister on the 4th April 1783. Lord Cadogan retained his family access to the highest political office in the land, as both he and the Duke were nephews of the late Lady Bentinck[11] who before her marriage to the Duke's uncle, Count Bentinck, was Lady Margaret Cadogan, younger daughter of the 1st Earl Cadogan. In November 1783 Fox introduced his India Bill, to take power from the East India Company and transfer it to the government. Reform was needed, but Fox's proposals were seen as an outrageous attempt to transfer the power of the Company to himself and his friends. The King had never liked Fox, notwithstanding that at one time he had been in love with his aunt, Lady Sarah Lennox[12], and he was keen, therefore, to rid himself of Portland's ministry. He could not, however, persuade enough members of the Commons to vote against the bill but when it went to the Upper Chamber, George III used his influence with the Lords, who threw out the proposal on the 17th December. The King then dismissed Fox and Lord North

Sir Robert Walpole with his family. Maria Skerrett is seated beside Sir Robert and behind her is Lady Mary Churchill on the arm of Horace Walpole

and appointed Pitt, aged 24, as his Prime Minister on the 7th December. No. 10 Downing Street had a new tenant who was to remain there for the next seventeen, mainly turbulent, years of the nation's history.

George was now, together with Emily, Charlotte and Henry, in the care of a nursemaid, Ann Collins, and the future of the Cadogan family at Caversham Lodge must, in 1785, have seemed assured. Then, 'in consequence of some unhappy connubial events (Lord Cadogan) sold land, house, furniture, wine in the cellar and, if we are to credit report, the very roast beef on the spit, to Major Marsac, for a sum of money one day before dinner.'[13] The nature of these 'unhappy' events is not recorded, but some clue may, perhaps, be gained from Lady

Cadogan's letter to her uncle, Horace Walpole, written later that same year.

Santon Downham
Monday November 14th

MY DEAR MR WALPOLE,

I just take up my pen to inform you that Mrs Turke died yesterday morning and that Lord Orford [Sir Robert Walpole's grandson – the 3rd Earl of Orford] is very well, except having got a wrench the other day when on horseback, for which he has had Doctor Norford's advices. I enter into all these particulars for fear the various reports that have already been spread here abouts should reach your ears and make you unwary, as for example I heard yesterday that he was gone mad and had sent for his lawyer to alter his will, but Biggleston went to Briwell this morning to enquire how he did, from us, and he had been out (for) an airing, but was going to lay down as the motion of the carriage gave him pain. He has two gentlemen with him. You will make what use you please of my intelligence and if you like to come here in order to go over to him, we shall be happy to see you when you may show him any attention you think proper without appearing to make a fuss, as you may be supposed only to come here in your way to Town, where you had proposed to go about this time.

Pray forgive this horrid scrawl, as it is the first letter I have written since my illness and that my nerves are hardly now equal to this task, though I am I hope gaining ground every day, yet I have not yet been able to venture out or get down to dinner. Best compliments to all your family, accept the same for yourself and believe me My Dear Mr Walpole,

Most Faithfully and Affectionately Yours,

M. CADOGAN

Whatever the reason, the family seat was now at Downham Hall, a spacious mansion of white Suffolk brick situated on the southern bank of the Little Ouse, twelve miles north from Bury St Edmunds and thirty miles south-west from Norwich, over the Norfolk border. The diarist who had waxed so enthusiastic about Caversham was less keen about Santon Downham.

The Family

We breakfasted at Brand, in Suffolk. All about that place is, I think, one of the most horrid countries I ever beheld, and near here is the new purchase of our Oxfordshire neighbour, Lord Cadogan, called Sandy (later Santon) Downham: indeed, nothing but sand is visible – no tree, or hardly a bush. The road styled Brand Sands, for about thirteen miles (is nothing but) deep sand over the horses' hoofs, but they are endeavouring to mend it by mixing it with chalk. But for his Lordship to sell so beautiful a spot as Caversham Park to purchase the above dreary wild spot is certainly beyond one's ideas.[14]

The Santon Downham estate comprised 3000 acres of farmland, 'chiefly warren, well stocked with rabbits'[15], and Lord Cadogan's land lay on either side of the Little Ouse which was navigable to Kings Lynn and The Wash. The transition from the manicured lawns of Caversham to the sandy wastes of Suffolk must have been something of a shock for Lady Cadogan. There were, nonetheless, local families in whose company new friendships and entertainment could be sought, including that of Sir Grey and Lady Cooper who lived at nearby Thurlo with their younger son and two daughters. The elder son, William, 19, was serving as an ensign in the 3rd Foot Guards, the former regiment of Lord Cadogan's eldest son, Charles. Sir Grey was a Whig and a former member of Parliament.

In March 1786 Lady Cadogan gave birth to another daughter who was christened Sophia, and at about that time the town home was removed from St James's Square across Piccadilly to 3, New Burlington Street. At the end of the Season, Lady Cadogan remained in London to sit for Sir Joshua Reynolds at his studio in Leicester Fields; the final sitting took place in mid-September. What should then have been an occasion for celebration, was marred by the death of little Sophia. The portrait[16] of a very wistful Lady Cadogan was shown at the Royal Academy summer exhibition in 1787 before removal to Downham Hall where it arrived in time for the birth of a further daughter, Louisa, on the 1st September. The other children were by now, aside from the four-year-old George,

Lady Cadogan (née Mary Churchill)

old enough to require a governess and a Berkshire cleric's daughter, Miss Armstrong, was taken into the household. As if in anticipation of a noisier country home, Lord Cadogan earlier in the year had taken a lease from Lord Walsingham of nearby Merton Hall in Norfolk. An annual feature of the Cadogan's social calendar in the country was a visit to Wolterton Hall, the home of Lady Cadogan's cousin Lord Walpole who, in 1789, was pleased also to entertain his third cousin

The Family

Captain Horatio Nelson of the Royal Navy and his wife Frances, familiarly known as Fanny. Captain Nelson at the time was on half-pay and awaiting a new command. Visits also continued to be exchanged with the Cooper family; Sir Grey had now been returned to Parliament as one of the members for Richmond in Yorkshire, while William Cooper had left the army, married, and was preparing for a new career in the church. The main topic of conversation on these occasions no doubt was the Revolution in France. Pitt and most of the leading politicians did not regard the French news as unwelcome, on the premise that a country riven by strife would be in no position to dominate European affairs as she had done in the past. Europe could now, perhaps, look forward to many years of peace, during which Britain would have an opportunity to repair the financial damage done by the costly and unsuccessful American War. A small minority positively welcomed the French Revolution in the hope that it would act as a catalyst for parliamentary reform in Britain; the Irish writer and English MP Edmund Burke, however, in his analysis of

Merton Hall

the turmoil, *Reflections on the Revolution in France,* published in November 1790, correctly prophesied that it would lead to great bloodshed and cruelty, the emergence of a dictator and a long war.

As French revolutionary fervour ran its course, the domestic hearth at Downham Hall remained, for the time being at least, undisturbed. George was now in his seventh year, and firmly in the tutelage of Miss Armstrong. There was, nonetheless, time to play on the river banks and to watch the fishing boats working from Lowestoft where Lord Cadogan had a coastal retreat for the better weather. Children generally were now being treated in a much more kindly way than earlier generations and there can be little doubt that George would have been told, for a small boy, exciting tales of the foreign sea-going adventures of his third cousin Captain Nelson, now living not so far away at Burnham Thorpe. Brother Henry was about to depart to Eton College for his formal education while Emily and Charlotte were very much the young ladies, taking a keen interest in their new baby brother, Edward. Lord and Lady Cadogan had quickly tired of the close confines of New Burlington Street and had moved to the comparative openness of 21, Hanover Square[17], a large house in the south-western corner regarded as 'the best piece of brickwork in the metropolis'. Their immediate neighbour at No. 20 was Welbore Ellis, a member of Parliament and a former Lord of the Admiralty and Treasurer of the Navy who was married to Lord Cadogan's cousin, Anne Stanley, a grand-daughter of Sir Hans Sloane. Hanover Square continued to exercise its charm until 1793 when a final move took Lord and Lady Cadogan to 41, Upper Grosvenor Street which had the advantage of its own stabling in the adjoining Reeves Mews. Before the move, however, the seeds were sown for the end of Lord Cadogan's marriage when Lady Cadogan took as her lover, the theological undergraduate and family friend William Cooper.

On mainland Europe the question of the French emigré

Hanover Square. No 21 is in the top right corner

nobles, many of whom had fled to the Holy Roman Empire, led France to declare war on Austria in April 1792. In July, Prussia allied herself to the Austrian cause and in the following month the Parisian sansculottes stormed the royal palace at the Tuileries. Thousands of French aristocrats who had remained in France were arrested and the guillotine became a feature of many French towns and cities during the ensuing September massacres. A second wave of noble emigrés left the country, France was proclaimed a Republic and the National Assembly, to the consternation of the remaining European monarchies, offered support to any people in revolt against its rulers. In November the French armies invaded the Austrian Netherlands and threatened to open the river Scheldt to world trade and to build up the port of Antwerp as a rival to Rotterdam and London; Britain had already shown in 1788 that, in entering the Triple Alliance with Holland and Prussia, it would not allow this to happen. On the 21st January 1793, Louis XVI

[25]

was guillotined on the Place de la Revolution, an act which met with international condemnation. The French now saw themselves as a nation under threat and as a result 'the old enemy' declared war on Britain and Holland on the 1st February and on Spain five weeks later, to embroil them all in the 'Revolutionary Wars'.

Pitt knew that the British Army was of insufficient strength to play a major rôle in a continental war and he relied, therefore, on Britain's allies of the First Coalition formed at the out-break of hostilities – Spain, Holland, Austria, Prussia and Russia – to do the greater part of the fighting with financial help from Britain; in theory, such powerful Allies would easily defeat the much smaller forces of France. In practice, however, there was little unity or purpose among them and they were poorly led. The French, on the other hand, were producing leaders of quality and the armed forces, although deprived of their Royalist officers, were fighting with much enthusiasm to defend the mother-country.

The war at sea hinged upon Pitt's intention to use the British Navy to blockade French ports, cut off France from colonial trading and help British troops in their operations against France and the French colonies. The outbreak of hostilities found the Royal Navy in good order; the fleet was ready for sea and it had a corps of officers unmatched in excellence and professional knowledge, including Howe, Hood, Collingwood, Jervis, Saumarez and Nelson, all of whom had been tried and tested in the bitter experience of the American War when the Navy, suffering from the economies of Lord North, had been unable to meet all of its commitments, resulting in the ignominy of Yorktown. Nelson was soon at sea again, in command of the *Agamemnon* and fighting the French in the Mediterranean. Nearer home shores, on the 28th May 1794 Admiral Lord Howe in command of a blockade squadron comprising 26 ships of the line, met a French squadron of equal strength off Brest, which had been sent out to escort a large convoy of merchantmen sailing from America with much needed grain. The ensuing engagement continued for six days and resulted in a tactical victory for Howe in what subsequently became known as 'The Glorious First of June'. The French lost seven ships of the line and 7000 men, dead, wounded and captured, while Howe's squadron sustained 1150 casualties. The grain ships nonetheless arrived safely in France.

In the quieter reaches of England, Lady Cadogan continued her affair with William Cooper who, having received a Lambeth Master of Arts degree, had been instituted as a prebendary of Rochester Cathedral. They met both in London and Lowestoft as suitable occasions arose while Mrs. Bull, recently awarded an annuity by Lord Cadogan, kept watch. With other more loyal servants in the household, however, discovery was inevitable and this came about in March 1794. The revelation was particularly hurtful for Lord Cadogan, as he had treated William Cooper with some generosity, and he

'The Glorious First of June', 1794

lost no time in issuing an action against him for 'criminal conversation' – a common law action against an adulterer. The matter was tried in the Court of King's Bench on the 3rd June by 'a special Jury of lawful and honest men' and Lord Cadogan was awarded £2000 in damages, which must have been a considerable embarrassment to the defendant with three young children to support, and whose father-in-law, against expectations, had recently died insolvent. On the 13th November, to add to the retributive burden, the Reverend Cooper was inhibited from holding his prebendal stall at Rochester and 'his deprivation and degradation were pending'.[18] Lord and Lady Cadogan, after sixteen years of marriage, now chose to live apart and at about this time the eleven-year-old George went away to school.[19]

The continental war ground on and, in October 1794, France invaded Holland and made another incursion into The Empire to capture Cologne, Andernach and Coblenz. These events persuaded Austria to sign an armistice on the 31st December and on the 5th April 1795 Prussia also made peace with France, followed by Holland on the 16th May and Spain on the 22nd July. Effectively, Britain now stood alone and it was at this juncture that the question arose as to George's future. Generally the matter would have been considered when a boy was fifteen or sixteen, and the choice for a younger son of a landed family would, in the normal course of events, rest between the army, the East India Company, politics and, after going to university, the church or the law. It was not unknown, however, for a spirited boy with thoughts of adventure, who found school life restricting, to seek his father's permission to join the Navy and this was likely the case with George. A naval career was out of the question for a son and heir as it was thought too dangerous and too demanding. Lord Uxbridge, for example, 'felt that the Navy was an unsuitable profession for his son and heir, and Paget (later the 1st Marquis of Anglesey) was considerably galled to see his younger brother William, when only fourteen, leave

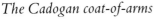

The Cadogan coat-of-arms

*Charles Cadogan, eldest son of
Charles and Frances Cadogan*

Westminster (School) before him to become a midshipman.'[20]
There was small chance, however, of George succeeding to
the barony as before him came the claims of his half-brothers
Charles and William and his brother Henry. Most boys destined for the Navy were at sea by the time they were 14 at the
latest and many more went afloat well before then; the future
Admiral Sir John Duckworth had fought in two major fleet
actions before his twelfth birthday. George was 12, intelligent, a little on the small side perhaps, but he had no doubt
learned to swim and to handle small craft on the Ouse and,
given the opportunity, probably enjoyed going on board the
herring luggers on his visits to Lowestoft. A naval career certainly seemed to square with George's likely inclinations and
abilities. Lord Cadogan, conscious of having already lost one
son at sea and the war now being fought, must have weighed
all these factors before informing George of his decision.

[29]

CHAPTER II

The King's Navy

George went on board His Majesty's frigate *Indefatigable* on Friday the 15th December 1795 at Plymouth, while the 46-gun warship was in dock undergoing a thorough repair, following a grounding the previous year off Cape Finisterre. It had not been difficult for Lord Cadogan to find him a berth as a First Class Volunteer with the commander, Captain Sir Edward Pellew, a large bluff but kindly Cornishman and a fine officer who had been knighted only the year previously and who 'was a great promoter of dancing and other sports'.[1] This was the golden age of patronage, that cement of society providing 'vertical links of mutual dependence and obligation'[2] and Lord Cadogan, whose house in Whitehall was presently occupied by Evan Nepean, Secretary to the Board of Admiralty, might prove a useful counter at some time in Pellew's advancement. As Pellew achieved higher rank he in turn would be expected to advance the careers of his own officers. He would also have had in mind his time as second lieutenant under George's half-brother Thomas, during Thomas's captaincy of the frigate *Licorne* in 1779, when they had spent the summer on the Newfoundland Station.

According to the Navy system of rating its ships, the *Indefatigable* was nominally a fifth-rate which generally included any warship having 32–44 guns. A ship with more than 100 guns (and a crew of 850 or more) was a first-rate. A second-rate had 90–98 guns, a third-rate 64–80, a fourth-rate 50–60, and a sixth-rate 20–30 guns. In practice, an admiral's flagship was usually a first- or second-rate and the majority of any fleet comprised third-rates ('seventy-fours'); there were few

The Indefatigable *fights the* Virginie, *April 1796*

fourth-rates and most frigates were fifth-rates. A 'ship of the line' was a warship large enough to lie in the line of battle and by convention, first- down to fourth-rates were reckoned as line-of-battle ships (rarely 'battleships'). The backbone of the Navy was its seventy-fours, which provided the fighting power, and its frigates, 'the eyes and ears of the fleet', of which there were 130 and 136 respectively in commission. The ambition of any volunteer worth his salt was to command a frigate or, better still, a ship of the line.

A volunteer was referred to as a 'young gentleman' and he was in effect the captain's apprentice. He might well be the captain's son or nephew or perhaps the son of a friend or patron. He was allowed £6 a year and the boy's parents provided his clothing which included two uniforms, a dress and an undress or informal suit, to mark his status as a would-be commission officer. A young gentleman could not expect to become a commission officer (the 'ed' was not added until much later) until he had passed his examination for lieutenant, and he would be unable to appear before the examining board until he was twenty years old and could produce certificates showing his name had been on ships' books for at least six years, two of which had been spent in the Petty Officer rating as a midshipman or master's mate. The status of a volunteer, in practical terms, was nonetheless unaffected by his rating which was dictated by chance or convenience. It was of no consequence if, as was to prove the case with George, a young gentleman was moved from volunteer to midshipman then to able seaman and eventually back to midshipman, for none of these titles had much bearing upon his actual duties. In practice he was growing in physique and experience, taking on greater responsibilities and coming to behave more like the commission officer he hoped one day to be.

For the time being, however, George was the new boy with much to learn and no doubt joining his first ship occasioned very similar thoughts and observations to those later recollected by a young midshipman of the day, also fresh from shore, when he went down the hatchway to look at the main deck:

Ye gods, what a difference! I had anticipated a kind of elegant house with guns in the windows; an orderly set of men; in short, I expected to find a species of Grosvenor Place, floating around like Noah's ark.

Here were the tars of England rolling about casks, without jackets, shoes or stockings. On one side provisions were received on board; at one port-hole coals, at another wood; dirty women, the objects of sailors' affections, with beer cans in hand, were everywhere conspicuous; the shrill whistle squeaked, and the voice of the boatswain and his mates rattled like thunder in my ears; the deck was dirty, slippery and wet; the smells abominable; the whole sight disgusting; and when I remarked the slovenly dress of the midshipmen, dressed in shabby round jackets, glazed hats, no gloves, and some without shoes, I forgot all the glory of Nelson, all the pride of the Navy, the terror of France, or the bulwark of Albion; and, for nearly the first time in my life, and I wish I could say it was the last, I took the handkerchief from my pocket; covered my face and cried like the child I was.

[32]

He then descended into the twilight world of the lower deck where he found the midshipman's berth which usually had only a few boys under fourteen years old, the majority being between twenty and thirty, with some forty years old or more:

It was noon, at which time the men and midshipmen dine, and consequently I found my companions at their scanty meal. A dirty tablecloth, which had the marks of the boys' fingers and the gentlemen's hands, covered the table. It had performed both offices of towel and tablecloth since Sunday.

A piece of half-roasted beef – the gravy chilled into a solid, some potatoes in their jackets, and biscuits in a japanned basket, with some very questionable beer, formed the comestibles.

The berth was about ten feet long by about eight broad; a fastened seat, under which were lockers, was built round the bulkhead; and the table, a fixture from sea lashings, was of that comfortable size that a man might reach across it without any particular elongation of the arm. A dirty-looking lad, without shoes or stockings, dressed in a loose pair of inexpressibles, fitting tight round the hips, a checked shirt, with the sleeves turned up to the elbows – his face as black as a sweep's, and his hands as dirty as a coalheaver's, was leaning against the locker, and acted in the dignified capacity of midshipmen's boy. Glass, a brittle material, and one which shows dirt both in the liquid and on its sides, was too expensive and too easily expended to be much used in the Navy. Cups answered their purpose and therefore cups were used. The soup-tureen, a heavy, lumbering piece of block-tin, pounded into shape, was, for the want of a ladle emptied with an ever-lasting teacup; the knives were invariably black, both on the handles and on the blades, and the forks were wiped in the table-cloth by the persons about to use them, and who, to save eating more than was required of actual dirt, always plunged them through the table-cloth to clean between the prongs. The table-cloth was changed on Saturdays. The rest of the furniture was not much cleaner: now and then an empty bottle served as a candlestick; and I have known both a shoe and quadrant-case used as a soup plate. It was in a habitation like this, 'a prison', as Mr. Johnson says, 'with the chance of being drowned,' that the sons of the highest noblemen were placed; and here, instead of the well-powdered lackey, the assiduous servant, or the eager attendant, he found but one almost shirtless boy to attend upon fourteen aspiring heroes – heroes who commanded by rights of years and strength, not by birth.

Such was the midshipman's and therefore the volunteer's lot, and when he sought the comfort of sleep on his first night he found that: 'A hammock served as a bed, and so closely were we all stowed in the war that the side of one hammock always touched that of another; fourteen inches being declared quite sufficient space for one tired midshipman to sleep in.'[3]

The *Indefatigable* was a *razé*, originally a ship of the line measuring approximately 150 feet along the main deck, with a beam, or maximum breadth, of some 45 feet, cut down by a deck due to operational requirements. She was therefore both larger and faster and more heavily armed than an ordinary frigate, making her too powerful for a French frigate to withstand and too fast for a French ship of the line to overtake. Launched in 1784 at Buckler's Hard on the River Beaulieu in Hampshire as a 3rd rate 64-gun ship of 1384 tons, she now carried 46 guns comprising twenty-six 24-pounders on the main deck, fourteen 18-pounders on the quarter deck and six 42-pounder carronades on the forecastle. These 'great guns', which were distributed equally on either side of the ship, took their description from the weight of the roundshot they fired. Smaller guns were carried for use in the ships' boats. There were three types of 24-pounders in general use; their barrels ranged in length from $9\frac{1}{2}$ feet to 6 feet and they weighed from $1\frac{1}{2}$ to $2\frac{1}{2}$ tons. The roundshot fired was some $5\frac{1}{2}$ inches in diameter with an extreme range of 3000 yards; the shot for an 18-pounder was just under 5 inches in diameter with a range similar to the 24-pounder. Roundshot had a tremendous power of penetration and at thirty yards, a typical range in battle, an 18-pounder shot could penetrate four oak planks $32\frac{1}{2}$ inches thick, driving a shower of potentially lethal splinters up to thirty yards. The Carronade, made by a Scottish firm, Carron Company, was a comparatively recent addition to a ship's guns. It had a much shorter barrel than the normal gun,

Gunners moving a carronade into position

it was light, had a wider bore and fired a heavier shot. The carronades were extremely effective at close range and were known, appropriately, as 'smashers'. The near-simultaneous fire of all guns on one side of the ship was known as a 'broad-side' which could be used with devastating effect. A warship was, essentially, a floating fortress with a capacity to carry enough powder, shot, food and water to enable her captain to keep her at sea, should the need arise, for more than three months. It no doubt seemed a lot longer to the ship's complement, given the generally cramped and spartan conditions on board, more especially during an Atlantic winter.

Pellew, who was now 38 with twenty-five years' service in the Navy, had command of a notional maximum complement of 276 men comprising a complex hierarchical structure of commission officers, warrant officers, petty officers, seamen, servants and, last but by no means least, a detachment of Marines. (The Marines did not receive their 'Royal' recognition until 1802.) The Navy was, however, so short of men within a year of the war beginning, that a captain had to strive very hard indeed to obtain a full crew, notwithstanding the Impress Service, which operated the notorious press gangs, and the Quota Acts which brought on board many a reluctant landman and merchant seaman. It was not unusual at this time for ships to leave port with something considerably less than a full complement.

The commission officers were the first, second and third lieutenants, while the principal warrant officers included the master (the fashionably named Mr. Pitt) responsible for navigation, the gunner, carpenter, and the surgeon. The master-at-arms, whose duty was to instruct the men in small arms drill together with some disciplinary responsibility, and the sailmaker were ranked 'inferior' warrant officer. Beneath them came the petty officers who, in addition to the master's mates and midshipmen, included the quartermasters and quarter gunners. The seamen, of course, were the largest group on board with an authorised maximum complement of 132, and they were divided into able seamen, ordinary seamen, and novices referred to as landmen. The Marine detachment numbered forty men under the immediate command of a lieutenant and they were expected to fight ashore if landing parties were needed or to act as snipers and sharpshooters during a close-fought sea battle.

The ship's captain was judge and jury to his men; his decision could bring them into battle and thus he had the power of life or death over everyone on board. Discipline for the crew was based upon thirty-six Articles of War: regulations laid down by the Board of Admiralty in London – the head of naval administration – which in certain instances such as mutiny or striking an officer, decreed death. The more common offences such as drunkenness and disobedience incurred a flogging of greater or lesser severity depending upon the whim of the captain, who was bound by few restrictions; he alone was ultimately responsible for his ship and for the well-being of all on board. In recognition of this heavy onus, the captain, as might be expected, was comparatively highly paid. He received the largest share of the sale proceeds of captured vessels – prize-money –and he was afforded the best quarters at the after end of the main deck, comprising a 'great cabin' which ran the width of the ship naturally lit by the stern lights, and two smaller cabins forward of this for dining and sleeping.

The rest of the ship's company lived on the lower deck where the only natural light and air was that which percolated down the hatches and companion way. At the after end was the gunroom (known as the wardroom in larger ships), a large cabin with several very small bunk-bed cabins which accommodated the lieutenants, the Marine officer, master, purser and surgeon. Forward of the gunroom were more small cabins for such as the bosun and gunner and one large cabin for the midshipmen which they shared with the young gentlemen volunteers. Forward again the Marines slung their hammocks to form a barrier between the officers and the seamen whose hammock space occupied most of the remaining deck area. The lower deck with the men off-watch sleeping in their hammocks was packed, dark, airless and to any unfortunate sailor so inclined, claustrophobic. The space beneath the lower deck, which when the ship was under fire was safely below the waterline, included the powder room, shot locker, main hold, magazine and the surgeon's 'cockpit'.

The repair, or refit, of the *Indefatigable* was proving extensive and accordingly Lady Pellew had come to stay at Plymouth while the work was carried out. On the 26th January the captain and his wife had accepted an invitation to dine and on arrival their host came to the side of the coach where Lady Pellew was sitting and inquired whether they had heard of the shipwreck under the Citadel. 'He had time to say but little more on the subject before Sir Edward opened the other door and disappeared.' The vessel which had been driven ashore was the *Dutton*, a large troop transport homeward bound from the West Indies which, in seeking shelter in Plymouth Sound, had been driven ashore by a violent gale beneath the heights of the Citadel adjacent to the Hoe. The *Dutton*'s masts were overboard and she was beating to pieces. On board were 400 troops, many of whom were sick with 'malignant fever', a number of women and the crew. One line had been fixed from ship to shore and a few of the more able-bodied men had been rescued; it was proving a slow business, however, and

The wreck of the Dutton

time was running out. George and others of the *Indefatigable* were about to witness their captain in action.

I observed with some admiration the behaviour of a Captain of a man-of-war, who seemed interested in the highest degree for the safety of these poor wretches. He exerted himself uncommonly, and directed others what to do on shore, and endeavoured in vain with a large speaking-trumpet to make himself heard by those on board; but finding that nothing could be heard but the roaring of the wind and sea, he offered anybody five guineas instantly who would suffer himself to be drawn on board with instructions to them what to do. And when he found that nobody would accept his offer, he gave an instance of the highest heroism: for he fixed the rope about himself and gave the signal to be drawn on board. He had his uniform coat on and his sword hanging at his side. I have not room to describe the particulars; but there was something grand and interesting in the thing: for as soon as they had pulled him into the wreck, he was received with three vast shouts by the people on board; and these were immediately echoed by those who lined the shore, the garrison-walls and lower batteries.

[38]

The first thing he did was to rig out two other ropes like the first:
which I saw him most active in doing so with his own hands. This
quickened the matter a good deal, and by this time two large open
row-boats were arrived from the Dockyard, and a sloop had with
difficulty worked out from Plymouth Pool. He then became active
in getting out the women and the sick, who were with difficulty got
into the open boats, and by them carried off to the sloop, which
kept off for fear of being stove against the ship or thrown upon the
rocks. He suffered but one boat to approach the ship at a time, and
stood with his drawn sword to prevent too many rushing into the
boat. After he had seen all the people out of the ship to about ten or
fifteen, he fixed himself to the rope as before, and was drawn
ashore, where he was again received with shouts. Upon my inquiry
who this gallant officer was, I was informed that it was Sir Edward
Pellew, whom I had heard the highest character of before, both for
bravery and mercy.

The soldiers were falling into disorder when Sir Edward went on
board. Many of them were drunk, having broke into the cabin and
got at the liquor. I saw him beating one with the flat of his broad-
sword, in order to make him give up a bundle he had made up of
plunder. They had but just time to save the men, before the ship was
nearly under water . . . the ship was washed all over as the sea rose –
she is now in pieces.[4]

Shortly afterwards the *Indefatigable*, with her repairs completed, sailed from Plymouth to Falmouth where she lay at her
moorings in Garrick Road for the rest of the winter. During
this time, Pellew lived at nearby Flushing and it was here in
late February that he received a letter[5] from the Earl Spencer,
First Lord of the Admiralty:

I did not fail on the earliest opportunity to state in the manner it
deserved to His Majesty your conduct in assisting the Dutton E.
Indiaman, and I have the sincerest satisfaction in having an express
Command from His Majesty to signify to you his very marked
approbation of it. His Majesty has been further pleased to add an
offer to you of the Rank & title of a Baronet of Gt. Britain as a more
publick testimony of the sense he entertains of your general good
Conduct and activity in his Service as well as more particularly for

the laudable Humanity and Spirit displayed by you on this occasion.

If, as I do not doubt, you should accept of this Mark of His Majesty's favour, you will be so good as to let me know by the Return of the Post the Place of your most usual Residence that I may take the proper steps for putting the Patent in Train through the several publick offices.

On the 5th March 1796, Sir Edward became Baronet of Treverry, which was not actually his 'most used Residence' but at the time it was the only landed property connected with the Pellew family.

There were two squadrons based on Falmouth as part of the Channel fleet; one was commanded by Pellew and as a result there were sometimes as many as ten frigates anchored off-shore.

... there would be sometimes a dozen men-of-wars' boats at the Quay at the same time, including the barges for the commanding officers, and the cutters, gigs, launches, and jolly boats on duty; the boats' crews mostly dressed in dashing marine trim, with blue jackets and trousers and bright scarlet waistcoats, overlaid with gilt buttons, in winter; and striped Guernsey frocks and white flowing trowsers in summer; while the little village literally sparkled with gold epaulets, gold lace hats, and brilliant uniforms.[6]

George no doubt enjoyed the nautical bustle of the Cornish port but the time was fast approaching for more serious business. He was no longer the newest face on board as the captain had just taken on muster another young gentleman, Henry Hart, from Uckfield in Sussex, who was two years older than George and a relative of Sir Percival Hart Dyke. Pellew's squadron, led by the *Indefatigable*, sailed on the 9th March and consisted of the frigates *Argo, Amazon, Concorde* and *Revolutionnaire*, the lugger *Duke of York* and three chasse-marées (small coastal vessels). It was not unusual for British ships to have French names; the *Concorde*, for example, had been captured from the French in 1783, and occasionally a French name was perpetuated when an earlier prize was replaced by a new

Captain Sir Edward Pellew

ship. The Squadron rounded Ushant and arrived off Belle Ile in the Bay of Biscay the following day, sailing then to Quiberon Bay where a French brig laden with salt was captured and sent back to England. The main objective was to land arms, ammunition and stores for the Chouans, the Breton Catholics who were in revolt against the French Government. The landings commenced on the 15th March and were completed by the 7th April, during which time the squadron wrought havoc among the merchant craft plying between French ports,

The scenes of
George Cadogan's
naval career from
1796 to 1802

taking or destroying nine small vessels at L'Orient and Rochefort. On the night of the 13th/14th April the squadron intercepted a French frigate, the 38-gun *Unité*, attempting to run
into Rochefort, and after a general chase it surrendered to the
guns of the *Revolutionnaire*.

Pellew did not return immediately to home port with his
prize and he cruised off Ushant before taking up station off the
Lizard. There on the 20th April he 'saw a strange sail on the
weather quarter' which did not answer his private signal. Pellew then ordered the *Revolutionnaire* and the *Argo* to escort the
captured *Unité* back to Plymouth while he, in the company of
the *Amazon* and *Concorde* all with colours hoisted and men
cheering, gave chase. George and his new friend, Henry Hart,

were about to have their first uncomfortable experience of naval warfare at close quarters.

The strange sail proved to be the 40-gun French frigate *Virginie*, four days out from Brest with 339 men on board, commanded by Captain Jacques Bergeret who, after striking his colours, reported to his fleet Admiral:

I have but just time enough to acquaint you with the disagreeable News of the taking of the *Virginie* by the English razé *Indefatigable* and two other frigates belonging to the squadron. I ought to keep quiet and wait, from those who will judge me, my justification, if I am susceptible of it; but my duty and my gratitude towards you obliged me to enter into particulars concerning that event, which will, I think, prove the impossibility I was in of preventing it.

At break of day, the 1st instant, [French Revolutionary Calendar] the men sent to look out gave me notice of nine sails to the NE, which course I was making to have a sight of the Lizard. I made more sail to reconnoitre them and at $\frac{1}{2}$ after Eight, being distant from them about $2\frac{1}{2}$ leagues and near eight leagues from the coast, I was convinced that five of them were frigates; the wind blowing then a fresh gale from the SE, I was chaced, but not being to windward of the *Indefatigable* that ship being even to the windward of the rest of the Enemies. I ran large to prevent his having that advantage over me. For the first hour his chace was unsuccessful whilst in the mean time she dropped the other frigates, but the wind experiencing a change successively in their direction and strength at 3.0 o'clock P.M. We were about half a league distant from the *Indefatigable*, being then as much favored as he, we dropped him a little till the beginning of the night, but my fore top gallant yard being carried away at the same instant, he fetched me again, leaving the other frigates at a great distance. The great moonlight kept me in sight of him till 11 o'clock 55 minutes when being in the impossibility of shunning him, I fired upon him my stern chaces but soon coming up with me quarter shot distance, he began to fire upon me, the wind being upon his quarter. Our first broad side did him a great deal of damage which however did not prevent him to come yard arm to yard arm, and there by the quickness of his fire, he did me the greatest damage. The main deckers are the only guns which I have been able to fire; after the first shots the men quartered on the forecastle and quarter deck left their situations and hid themselves except the captains; being obliged to give those guns over, it is not without blows that I have been able to make them secure their guns. The main deck however has been well fought, the *Indefatigable* bearing up so as to put his bowsprit into my shrouds, I made the motion to engage with the wind ahead but either through manoeuvre or damage which he has sustained, he hove all aback and received in that position two broadsides which cut his gaff, his mizen top mast and crossjack yard – and I immediately, favored by the smoke, bore up to get away, without being able to go more than three or four cable lengths from him; he soon got to rights again and returned upon me with the greatest impetuosity.

My heart bleeds to tell you that I was forced to take musquets to make use of them against the top men and to send a midshipman to strike them. I have been often left alone with the officer charged with the manoevre, forced to jump down and with the help of the Master at Arms and some other Masters, to haul on the ropes. At a $\frac{1}{4}$ after 1, I lost my mizen mast and the *Indefatigable* bringing again his bowsprit in my shrouds, I once more luffed up in the wind on purpose to rake him by the bows which he prevented by hauling his wind – his sails being less damaged than the *Virginie*'s who had then but her fore and fore top sails up – he went ahead of me, which made me resolve to come to the Wind and by that means to rake him by the stern, when my main top mast fell across the main yard which with the mizen mast prevented me from firing but three guns. It was not for a long time in his power to fire upon us, he bore up to get at a greater distance to engage anew. I was myself obliged

A ship's gun

to use the hatchets to clear away the wreck of the masts which falling, the deck was almost always of service until two o'clock, when a frigate coming within a pistol shot, without however firing but in such a position as rendered it impossible for us to bring a single gun to bear upon him, the pieces of my fore and fore top sails remaining not being sufficient to steer the frigate and the third of the enemies coming up fast towards us, I struck my colours, not being able to defend myself any longer, having besides four feet in the hold. I thought at first to have lost a great many men but I could be sure but of the death of 13 and about 30 wounded, 17 of whom dangerously; the loss of so few people might bespeak a weak resistance if the state in which the *Virginie* is did not prove the contrary. I have however my conscience as a consolation, but I appear in a disfavorable light; my misfortune ought not to make me forget to mention honourably my officers, who without the least doubt were worth a better fate than that of falling into captivity. The Midshipmen are commendable as well as the 1st Masters and part of the Ship's Company, who as well as myself had the discontent of seeing a great many others not imitate them. The fore mast is hardly able to keep up, and with all the reparation made to the *Virginie* and the finest weather in the world, she leaks at the rate of 36 Inches an hour. The *Indefatigable* besides the damage mentioned before lost her fore top sail yard and her main top mast. She has kept almost whole her fore sail and her mizen only.

I will never forget this misfortune of mine but my existence would be an easy sacrifice if I had not to fear the loss of your esteem and that of my bread.

I am etc etc

People will not easily be persuaded that for all the damage suffered by the *Indefatigable* she has but one man wounded.[7]

On the 24th April the *Concorde* was ordered to tow the *Virginie* into Plymouth, where the *Indefatigable* arrived three days later in order to refit. Her stay on this occasion was not prolonged and on the 7th June she was at sea again cruising with the squadron on station between Ushant and Lizard Point.

In England, meanwhile, there was more strife, albeit of a

domestic nature, when Lord Cadogan 'exhibited a Libel' in the Consistory Court of the Bishop of London against Lady Cadogan, which resulted in his obtaining a 'Definite Sentence of Divorce' on the 15th June 1796. Lady Cadogan, with her substantial marriage settlement at stake, fought back and appealed on the 1st July to the Court of Arches, a superior ecclesiastical court, but without success. To complete the separation, Lord Cadogan then obtained a Private Act of Parliament[8] to dissolve the marriage and to prevent any 'spurious Issue' being imposed on him. The Act also enabled Lord Cadogan to marry again should he so wish and there was a specific declaration that the children born during the marriage 'shall be legitimate and inheritable to the Titles Honours Manors Lands Tithes Tenements and Hereditaments of Lord Cadogan'. The former Lady Cadogan now reverted to her maiden name and was 'barred and excluded from all Dower Free Bench and Thirds at the Common Law.' In simpler words, she left the marriage without any pecuniary benefit of substance. Mary Churchill now departed to take up residence with her parents, leaving Lord Cadogan to continue with his political life and the development of the Santon Downham estate where a major tree-planting programme was under way. The children, leave aside the two youngest, were now quite grown up. Emily was 18; Henry, still away at school, was 16 and contemplating a career in the Army; and Charlotte was 15. Louisa now 9 and Edward 7, were both in the care of Miss Armstrong who remained at Downham Hall as Governess.

The fine detail of his parents' parting was unknown to George who in any event had more than enough to occupy him, learning about life afloat. Pellew was 'particularly attentive' to the educational training of his young gentleman. George had regularly to attend upon the schoolmaster, an 'inferior' warrant officer, who was appointed 'to employ his time (in part) in instructing the Volunteers in writing, arithmetic and navigation, and in whatever may contribute to render them proficients', while on other occasions the boatswain, the principal warrant officer, was teaching him how to knot and splice.

A much more hazardous, and in the normal course of events, daily occurrence, was 'exercising aloft'. Warships had three masts – the mizzen mast, main-mast and fore mast – and each of these carried three levels of sail named according to the mast; hence, for example, mizzen top-sail, main top-sail and fore top-sail; the highest level comprised the top-gallants. These woven flax sails, not gleaming white but something nearer to 'a warm tint of raw umber', were moved by a network of cables, rigging and pulleys operated by able seamen to provide the motive power for the vessel, while the ship was steered mainly by the effect of the ship's wheel on the rudder. The volunteers, working a hundred feet above the deck, were taught how to unfurl and then reef the smallest sails, the top-gallants and the mizzen topsail, and the officers were urged to

Sailors taking in a reef

'raise an emulation in them, to outdo those of other ships'. It was considered indispensable for young gentleman to work aloft with the topmen and some of the less sure-footed were killed. The survivors, however, who went on to command knew precisely what they were ordering their seamen to do.

On the 8th October, Spain joined forces with the French, who were now also allied to the Dutch, and declared war on Britain, hoping to gain something out of the general conflagration that, with Austria returned to the conflict, engulfed Europe. Napoleon Bonaparte, a former artillery officer in the Bourbon Army which he joined in 1785 when he was 17, had risen meteorically to command the French Army of Italy in the preceding March, since when, 'leaping over mountains as if they had been mole heaps', he had inflicted two major defeats upon the Austrians who were now on their knees. An embargo had been placed on all Spanish shipping and as a result the *Indefatigable* and the remainder of the squadron spent three months operating off the coast of Spain where Pellew took half-a-dozen prizes in the region of Corunna, before returning to Plymouth for refitting. In December he returned to station off Ushant with orders to keep a close watch on Brest where, it was suspected, the French were preparing an expeditionary force for Ireland in the hope of promoting a rebellion there. The French fleet sailed on the night of the 16th December and Pellew despatched his lugger to Falmouth the following morning with news of this for transmission to the Admiralty in London. There then followed an extraordinary series of mishaps on both sides with the result that having reached Bantry Bay in south-west Ireland, the French fleet abandoned the enterprise and returned virtually unopposed to Brest where, save stragglers, it arrived on the 14th January. In the meantime, the *Indefatigable*, together with the *Amazon* and the *Duke of York*, had returned southward to the Spanish coast. George had survived his first full year at sea; he was shortly, however, to see the more brutal side of life in the King's Navy.

[48]

CHAPTER III

Mutiny

The new year of 1797 opened well for Pellew's squadron with the capture of two prizes off the Spanish coast. At a time when the rate of pay for a captain in command of a frigate was eight shillings a day and that for an ordinary seaman was nineteen shillings a month, prize money was keenly sought and was on occasion the cause of much acrimony and litigation. Prize money arose from the capture of enemy warships which, all being well, were purchased on behalf of the Admiralty. Alternatively, a lucky captain might take an enemy merchant ship, hopefully with a valuable cargo, which would be disposed of by an Admiralty court. The total prize money was divided into eighths and then shared out so that the commanding admiral, of station or fleet as the case might be, received one-eighth and the captain of the ship two-eighths. The lieutenants, master, surgeon and Marine officer shared an eighth; the principal warrant officers, master's mates, chaplain and admiral's secretary had an eighth; midshipmen, inferior warrant officers, mates of principal warrant officers (e.g., the surgeon's mate) and Marine sergeants had an eighth, while the rest of the ship's company shared two-eighths. As a measure of value, about this time the capture of a seaworthy enemy frigate of 32 guns was worth more than thirty-five year's pay for the captain, four year's pay for the lieutenants, and about a year and a half's pay for each able and ordinary seaman. If other ships helped take the prize they joined in the share as did any ship that was simply 'in sight', the theory being that its mere presence might have caused or contributed to the enemy ship striking. Pellew's hopes of a landed estate were gradually coming to fruition and George was earning a useful supplement to his weekly wage of half-a-crown.

The 13th January found the *Indefatigable* in company with the *Amazon* in passage for England and 150 miles south-west of Ushant. At a quarter to one in the afternoon, a sail was sighted on the port bow, 'steering under easy sail for France'. The English frigates, inshore of her, made sail at once to cut her off. Pellew subsequently reported: 'The wind was then at West blowing hard, with thick hazey weather. I instantly made the signal to the *Amazon* for a General Chace and follow'd it by the signal that the Chace was an Enemy.' Pellew was unaware at this time as to what sort of ship he was chasing. She was in fact the *Droits de l'Homme*, a French 74-gun ship of the line which, given the opportunity, might be expected to sink him with one broadside. The *Indefatigable* drew ahead and at three o'clock the *Amazon* was three or four miles astern; at ten minutes to four, Pellew beat to quarters and cleared for action and the French followed suit. The *Droits de l'Homme* was one of the returning stragglers from Bantry Bay and she was packed with some 700 troops. Built to a new experimental design and so being lower in the water, her captain, Commodore Jean Raimond Lacrosse, quickly discovered that the rough weather prevented him from using his lower deck guns.

... at 4 p.m. the *Indefatigable* had gain'd sufficiently upon the chace for me to distinguish very clearly that she [the *Droits de L'Homme*] had two tiers of guns, with her lower deck ports shut. She had no poop, and according to my judgment she was a French ship en razée. At ¼ before 5 I observ'd with considerable regret that she had carried away her fore and main topmasts. The *Indefatigable* at the same time lost her steering sail booms; the ship at this time was going 11 or 12 knots, blowing very hard and a great sea. I foresaw from this that the escape of the enemy under her lower masts only, in a stormy night of 14 hours continuation, should her defence prove obstinate, was very possible, and I believed that as a ship of large force she would be induced to persevere in her resistance from the expectation that we should be apprehensive of entangling ourselves upon a lee shore with the wind dead upon it. The instant she lost her topmasts I reduc'd my sails to close reef'd topsails and at 15 minutes before 6 we brought the Enemy to close action. . .

The two warships had now hoisted their respective colours and the damage to both had allowed the *Amazon* to come up and to join in the action.

. . . at this moment the *Amazon* appear'd astern and gallantly supplied our place but the eagerness of Capt'n Reynolds to second his friend had brought him up under a press of sail and after a well supported and close fire for a little time, he unavoidably shot ahead also. The Enemy, who had nearly effected running me on board, appear'd to be much larger than the *Indefatigable* and from her very heavy fire of musquetry I believe was very full of men, and this fire was continued until the end of the action with great vivacity, although he frequently defended both sides of his ship at once.

With 700 or so troops on board, the French would certainly have no shortage of muskets.

As soon as we had replaced some necessary rigging and the *Amazon* had reduced her sail, we commenced a second attack, placing ourselves, after some raking broadsides, upon each quarter and this attack, often within pistol shot was by both ships unremitted for above five hours, when we sheer'd off to secure our masts. . .

The two frigates broke off the action at 2 o'clock the following morning to clear wreckage and effect some urgent repairs. Just after three o'clock the attack was resumed, both frigates attacking at once. 'The ship was full of water, the cockpit half-leg deep, and the surgeon absolutely obliged to tie himself and patient to the stanchions to perform an amputation.' Fighting continued throughout the night, which was moonlit but overcast, and due to a combination of circumstances nobody knew exactly where they were.

. . . altho she was running for her own ports, yet the confidence I felt in my knowledge of the coast of France forbade me to listen for a moment to any suggestions of danger therefrom. I placed also some considerable reliance that her commander would not voluntarily sacrifice his ship and his crew by running her for a dangerous part of the coast and I promis'd myself to see the day before we should have run down our distance, but in fact every creature was too earnestly and too hardly at work to attend exactly to the run of the ship. I believe ten hours of more severe fatigue was scarcely ever experienced. The sea was high, the people on the main deck were up to their middles in water, some guns broke their breechings four times over, and some drew the ring-bolts from the sides, many of them repeatedly drawn immediately after loading. All our masts were much wounded, the main topmast completely unrigg'd, and sav'd only by uncommon alacrity. . .[1]

By seven o'clock on the morning of the 14th January, Pellew found that he was 'embayed on a lee shore, in as dangerous a position as any man could wish to avoid.' He immediately wore ship to the southward and ten minutes later, in growing daylight, he discovered the French ship dismasted, lying on a sandbank with the surf breaking over her – a total wreck. Ten days later, after limping into Falmouth, the *Indefatigable*, 'considerable damaged in hull, masts, and rigging' and 'making a great deal of water', arrived at Plymouth dockyard for extensive refitting. By now, it was known that the *Amazon* had also gone aground, not far from the *Droits de l'Homme*, in Audierne Bay twenty-five miles south of Brest. The *Amazon's* complement had been taken prisoner, while the French had lost 103 killed during the fighting and another 217 in the wreck. The *Indefatigable*, leading a comparatively charmed life, suffered no fatalities and nineteen wounded. On his report of the action, Pellew wrote that 'little Cadogan is a most delightful boy. I think he promises to be everything the heart can wish. He is stationed on the Lower Deck where I assure you, my lord, he was my friend. He stood the night out in his shirt and kept himself warm by his exertions. I cannot say too much in his praise!'

Given the necessary prerequisites of sufficient leave and

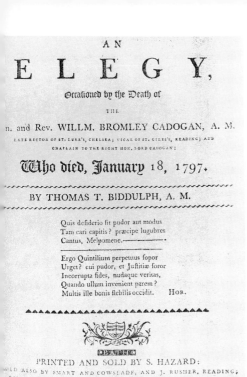

itle page of an Elegy for William Cadogan   *The Reverend William Cadogan*

money, Plymouth was a favourite port for both officers and men. Those with an inclination could seek distraction in the bars, inns and brothels, while others would take themselves off for a spell of home life. George chose to travel home on the London mail coach and he arrived at Upper Grosvenor Street at the end of January to find his father in mourning for his half-brother William who, following an 'inflammation of the bowels', had died at his home in Reading two weeks earlier, having just celebrated his 53rd birthday. William had been dedicated to his calling and was much admired for the

beautiful regularity of his conduct, and strict improvement of his time, rising constantly both in summer and winter, at six in the morning, and excepting his attendance at breakfast and family prayer, continuing always in his study till 12; then riding about two hours and visiting that part of his flock which was at a distance. In the afternoon he visited the sick and distressed in the town ...[3]

[53]

This sombre event was soon overlaid by the news of what came to be known as the battle of Cape St Vincent, fought two weeks after William's death. The French, in concert with their allies, had planned a triple naval assault upon Britain. On the 14th February the Spanish Mediterranean fleet, with 27 ships of the line led by a four-decker 130-gun flagship commanded by Don José de Cordova, was on its way to Brest to unite with the French fleet when it was met off Cadiz by a squadron of Vice-Admiral Sir John Jervis's Mediterranean fleet with the 100-gun flagship *Victory* supported by 15 ships of the line. One of them was the *Captain* with Nelson, now advanced to Commodore, on board. The Spanish fleet was split into two groups and only a very bold independent action by Nelson prevented them coming together which, in the result, gave the British squadron a resounding victory. The Spaniards lost four ships – ten more were badly damaged – and 5000 men dead, wounded or captured by the time Cordova was able to run into Cadiz. There Jervis, although having five of his ships badly damaged and 300 men lost, proceeded to blockade him. It was a timely victory which saved Britain

The Battle of Cape St Vincent, 1797

from possible invasion and a grateful King conferred an earldom on Jervis, who aptly chose 'St Vincent' for his title; Nelson was promoted Rear-Admiral and created a Knight of the Bath.

The *Indefatigable*, now fully repaired with a newly painted hull, departed from Plymouth for Falmouth on the 2nd March where George returned to ship. Pellew collected his squadron; the frigate *Greyhound* commanded by his brother Captain Israel Pellew, the *Revolutionnaire*, the lugger *Argus* and the cutter *Sally*, and returned to blockade duty off Brest. Six weeks later the Channel fleet anchored at Spithead, the roadstead between Portsmouth and the Isle of Wight, mutinied due to the sailors' grievances over inadequacy of pay and provisions. The Admiralty, conscious of new invasion threats from France and Holland, treated with the mutineers and as a result the monthly wages of ordinary seamen rose to 23s 6d and those of able seamen to 29s 6d, and measures were adopted to rectify faults in the distribution and quality of rations.

The Channel fleet was at sea again, its spirit recovered, on the 17th May, but by now ripples of discontent had spread to the fleet's anchorage at the Nore in the Thames estuary and to the *Indefatigable*. Only Pellew's long experience of Navy life enabled him to placate his men who, in their case, were more concerned about the tardy payment of prize money; his dictum to George was that 'you can never die so well, as on your own deck quelling a mutiny and now, if a man hesitate to obey you, cut him down without a word'.[3] The mutiny at the Nore petered out in the face of Admiralty determination not to grant any further concessions. In view of the fact that sister ships had been fired upon the ringleader, Richard Parker, was arrested, tried and hanged at the yardarm. Later, thirty-six other mutineers were also executed.

In October, the threat posed by the Dutch fleet was removed by the battle of Camperdown off the Dutch coast when a British squadron under Admiral Adam Duncan, after a bloody fight, took nine out of a total of sixteen enemy ships. Later that month, however, this advantage was offset when the Austrians once again made peace with France. The *Indefatigable* was newly employed making a survey of St Mary's Road, Scilly, and reporting on the possibilities of its being used as an anchorage for the Channel fleet. It was during this employment, on the 2nd January 1798, that George, now fourteen, received petty officer rating as a midshipman. By March the survey was completed and the *Indefatigable* in company with three other frigates was returned to blockade duty off Scilly with orders to 'intercept and destroy or capture anything that may be moving' between there and Ushant.

Life on board, awaiting sight of an enemy sail, followed a steady routine. At sea, all warships kept what were known as 'watches' where the seamen and petty officers were divided into two groups, the starboard and larboard (portside) watches. One whole watch was on deck at all times, night and day, and each watch lasted four hours except for the two 'dog watches' which lasted between four o'clock and eight o'clock in the evening. There were, therefore, seven watches in the day; an odd number which ensured that the duties of each watch continually varied. The changing of the watch was marked by the ship's bell which sounded every half-hour at the turn of a sand-glass kept by a petty officer, usually the quartermaster of the watch, and at eight bells the watch changed; the officer of the watch was usually one of the lieutenants or the master. The only men who could expect to sleep through the night in normal conditions, referred to as 'idlers', were the non-seamen officers including the surgeon, purser and carpenter and their subordinates. Whether the captain slept undisturbed depended upon the exigencies of the night.

At sunrise the ship went to quarters (battle-stations) and two lookouts were sent aloft to scan the horizon for enemy sails; given an 'all clear', the captain ordered the ship's company about its business. The daily cycle in summer began at 4 a.m. with the off-watch men being called, the men at the

A flogging

wheel and the lookouts being changed; a frigate in wartime
had at least six lookouts on deck at night. The idlers were
called and the cook lit the galley fire and made preparations for
breakfast while the carpenter sounded the 'wells' to check the
water level. A check was made of guns and rigging and the
duty watch scrubbed the upper deck and polished the brass-
work. The off-watch were then called to lash and stow their
hammocks and to clean the lower deck. At eight o'clock the
hands were piped to breakfast consisting, perhaps, of gruel
with bread and a little butter and cheese washed down with
'coffee' made from burnt breadcrumbs. Divisions were held at
half-past nine when the men paraded with their lieutenants
and midshipmen and the Marines with their officer.

It was now that any floggings were meted out, witnessed
by the whole ship's company, in the hope of deterring other
potential offenders. Lashings were awarded summarily by the
captain usually in multiples of twelve and would generally
range in number from 12 for drunkenness up to perhaps 72 for

desertion. The punishment was administered by one, or more if necessary, of the boatswain's (bosun's) mates using the 'cat of nine tails', a whip with an inch-thick rope handle, two feet long, and nine tails or lashes of similar length made of line a quarter of an inch in diameter. Only for theft were the nine tails knotted. The same cat was never used twice and to add to the awfulness of the occasion, it was carried in a specially stitched red baize bag. Flogging was a rough-and-ready form of 'justice' but viewed in context there was no alternative if a captain was to maintain discipline. 'The fact was that living, and still more sailing, in the crowded and dangerous environment of a ship required a high degree of self-discipline, and those who had not learnt it, or would not learn, were a burden on their shipmates.'[4] Floggings were few and far between on board the *Indefatigable* as Pellew was a fair captain with, perhaps more importantly, an instinct for prize money.

Divisions over, the duty watch would likely be practising their gun drill which consisted chiefly of loading, running out and (sometimes) firing the guns as quickly and reliably as possible. A frigate captain, with no guns on the lower deck where the off-watch might be in their hammocks, would aim to clear for action in five minutes. Time would also have to be allotted for bringing down sails for repair, small arms practice, fire-fighting drill, painting, whitewashing (especially on the lower deck) and blacking the guns, shot and rigging. Relief all round, therefore, at half-past-eleven when the order was given to 'clear decks and up spirits' for the first part of the day's grog – watered rum – followed by dinner at noon comprising, in the main, ship's biscuit and either salt beef or salt port with water or perhaps beer to drink. The officers usually drank wine and on occasion they were able to supplement the basic fare with fresh meat, eggs and milk provided by livestock, poultry, pigs and perhaps cattle kept in a manger at the forward end of the main deck. At half-past-twelve the duty watch exercised or worked and at two o'clock on Mondays, Wednesdays and Fridays, bread was issued.

[58]

The second part of the day's grog was issued at 4 o'clock and shortly after came the order to 'clear decks'. Half-an-hour before sunset the ship went to quarters and there was an inspection of both men and guns by the captain or first lieutenant. At dusk the masthead look-outs came down and six more men were placed round the ship, each to watch a particular section of the horizon. 'Down hammocks' was piped at eight o'clock to coincide with the changing of the watch, followed by 'ship's company's fire and lights out'. The officers had another two hours candlelight and the last order of the day, at ten o'clock, was 'gunroom lights out'. Sunday and Thursday were to some extent 'special days' at sea when the men were required to shave and put on clean shirts and trousers; Saturday afternoons were generally set aside for mending clothes and on the Sabbath there was opportunity to relax and to join in the hymn singing at divine service when the Captain might preach a sermon or read the Articles of War to the ship's company.

The *Indefatigable* continued cruising off Scilly and Ushant until the 17th July when she returned to Plymouth for a refit which kept her in dock until the end of October.

On the 19th May, Bonaparte, with the aim of conquering Egypt as a gateway to India, had sailed from Toulon with the 'Army of the Orient', escorted by the French Mediterranean fleet under Vice-Admiral François Brueys. After the general had landed at Alexandria, Brueys proceeded to anchor in Aboukir Bay, at the mouth of the River Nile. A British squadron under Nelson, who had lost his right arm the previous year in an action against the Spanish at Santa Cruz on the island of Tenerife (one of the Canaries), was sent in pursuit and succeeded in bringing the French to battle there on the 1st and 2nd August. The battle of the Nile gave Nelson a great victory and left Britain in control of the Mediterranean; Bonaparte's army in Egypt was stranded and at the end of December Britain formed the Second Coalition against France with

Austria, Russia, Naples, Portugal and Turkey. This proved
even shorter lived, however, than the First Coalition and after
initial success by the Austrian and Russian armies, a British
and Russian expedition failed in the mud of Holland, which
led to Russia withdrawing from the Coalition.

George's commander, in the meantime, had received a
nasty shock in the form of a letter[5] from Earl Spencer, the
First Lord of the Admiralty:

> The extensive Promotion of Flag Officers which His Majesty has
> been please to authorize me to make brings you so high on the
> Captains List, that it is no longer consistent with the ordinary prac-
> tice of the Service that you should continue to serve in a Frigate: I
> have therefore given you an appointment to the *Impetueux* as being
> the most active and desirable Line of Battle Ship which the arrange-
> ment on this occasion enabled me to select for you, and I have no
> doubt but that you will in this new line of service continue to gain as
> much credit as you have already, by the acknowledgement of every
> one who knows you, obtained.

Adm'ty 15 Feb: 1799

Pellew was very content with the *Indefatigable*. After four
years together the ship's company was moulded to his liking;
with a squadron to command he held the title of Commodore
and, more importantly, he could act more of less independent-
ly with, as results had shown, excellent prospects of prize
money. This apparent promotion would deprive him of all
these benefits and leave him just another captain in the Channel
fleet at Spithead under the orders of a man he loathed, Vice-
Admiral Lord Bridport (formerly Sir Alexander Hood).
Additionally, he knew that the *Impetueux*, a 74-gun ship captured from the French at the battle of the 'Glorious First of
June', had a major defect – a notoriously malcontent crew.
Pellew protested without success and to make matters worse
he was not permitted to take with him anyone from the *Indefatigable* – whose loyalty to him would be certain – apart from
young gentlemen. 'Little Cadogan may have been and doubt-

[60]

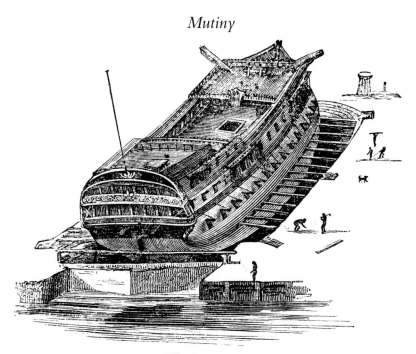

The Impetueux

less was, a delightful boy, but Pellew's need was for Petty Officers of another kind.'[6]

Pellew left the *Indefatigable*[7] at Plymouth on the 28th February, taking George and Henry Hart with him; he read his commission on board the *Impetueux* at Spithead on the 10th March. The two young gentlemen were both now sufficiently experienced to be, if nothing else, valuable 'ears and eyes' for their captain, who could only hope to bring the crew into line by watchfulness and severity. George was initially entered on the ship's muster as able seaman until the 15th March when he was again rated as midshipman. Pellew weighed anchor and sailed to Cawsand Bay, south-west of Plymouth Sound, where he punished three seamen with twenty-four lashes each for insolence and two others with a dozen each for drunkenness. From now on punishments came thick and fast. On the 25th May, after joining the fleet off Ushant, the *Impetueux* with three other ships went into Bearhaven Harbour in Bantry Bay to take on fresh water, and while moored there Pellew set the hands to paint the sides, which evidently exacerbated the situation. Three men received a dozen and two more twenty-four lashes for drunkenness, disobedience, or both. Then, two days later, four more men were flogged. On the 30th May, when the signal was made to unmoor, the crew mutinied. Pellew had gone to his cabin to dress when:

Hearing a great noise, I instantly ran out, and on my appearance the noise was much increased, the people, about two or three hundred, still pressing aft, and crying out, 'One and all, one and all; a boat – a boat.' I asked what was the matter, and was answered by Samuel Sidney (1st), and Thomas Harrop, and others, who were foremost in complaining of hard usage, flogging etc., and muttered something about a letter to Lord Bridport, which I repeatedly and vehemently asked for, saying on my honour I would carry it myself, or send an officer with it. To all this there was a constant cry of 'No – no – no! a boat of our own!' and the more I endeavoured to pacify them, and bring them to reason, the louder the noise became; many saying – Sidney, Harrop, and Jones, particularly – 'We will have a boat; d––, we'll take one.' This convinced me they were determined to go the greatest lengths, and was more than either my patience or my duty permitted me to bear. I only answered 'You will, will you!' and flew into my cabin for my sword, determined to support the King's service and my own authority, and to kill Sidney or Harrop, who were addressing me, and appeared to be the leaders. Happily that measure became unnecessary. . .

While Pellew was arming himself, the carpenter had gone below and returned with swords for some of the other officers, at which point Pellew reappeared carrying his sword. By now the captain of Marines was on the quarter-deck with some of his men. Faced with determined resistance the mutiny collapsed and Pellew, after securing nine of the ringleaders, drove the other men below. The *Impetueux* rejoined the fleet the following morning and shortly afterwards she sailed as one of a squadron to reinforce the Mediterranean fleet commanded by Lord St Vincent. It was not, therefore, until the 19th June that the mutineers faced a court martial on board the *Prince* at Port Mahon on Minorca, when three of the men were condemned to death and five others to be flogged round the fleet. On the morning of the 21st May at nine o'clock, with the ship's company assembled, 'Sam Sydney, Will Jones and Thos. Harrop (Seaman) were hanged at the yard Arm and at 10 their bodies were committed to the Deep.' If any emphasis was needed, Pellew then read the Articles of War. Less than twenty-four hours later: 'A.M. at 7 made the Sig'l for punishment. The following men were punished along side the *Impetueux, Prince, Triumph, Formidable,* – John Smith with 200 lashes, Law. Rhodes, Mich. Pennell, W. McAram, Stephen Walford, 100 lashes each.'[8]

The total number of lashes was divided by the number of ships present and the prisoners rowed from ship to ship, to the accompaniment of a slow drum beat, to receive the apportioned number, watched by the ship's crew. According to one eye-witness, after two dozen lashes 'the lacerated back looks inhuman; it resembles roasted meat burnt nearly black before a scorching fire.'[9] The *Impetueux* was now 'restored to quietness', although it was never a happy ship like the *Indefatigable* – and punishments were fairly frequent. Pellew's ship returned to the Channel fleet and the exacting task of blockading Brest.

CHAPTER IV

A Lieutenancy

Mary Churchill sat with her adviser Mr. Thomas Lewis at Grays Inn to settle the detail of her Will.[1] It was October 1799 and she would in a matter of months celebrate, or perhaps rue, her fiftieth birthday. She continued to live at the Churchill family homes in London and Kent and she received periodic visits from the children. Emily had come of age in May and Charlotte was eighteen. Henry was a lieutenant in the army and looked most gallant in his uniform. George was afloat, while Louisa and Edward continued their upbringing at Downham Hall.

Aside from her personal possessions, Mary's financial wealth was small enough and comprised £900 of three per cent Consolidated Bank annuities and an expectation of £2000, upon her father's death, arising from her mother's marriage settlement. Her first thought was to leave the greater part of that money to her 'beloved child' Edward but after much heart searching Mary decided that it should go to her 'faithful and most valued Friend the Reverend William Cooper', who would also receive her books, china, plate and her blue stone diamond ring. Mr Cooper who had resigned from his office at Rochester Cathedral following the divorce, would also act as Executor. Mary's 'much esteemed Friend and Servant' Mrs Bull would have £200 of the Consolidated Bank annuities with the remainder going to Edward. The girls would, of course, have her jewellery. Emily would have her mother's diamond necklace and earrings, Charlotte would have the two best diamond stars and the pearl bracelets, while to Louisa would go one diamond star and the large pearl necklace together with 'her Uncle General George Churchill's picture'. There was nothing in particular to leave to Henry and George; they seemed now so independent and in any event would be provided for by their father. Mary did not feel inclined to make provision for her final resting place; this would have to take care of itself. Mr Lewis finished his notes and escorted his client to her waiting carriage for the return journey to Grosvenor Street.

Lord Cadogan, now 71, increasingly preferred the peace of his estate at Santon Downham where his new plantations were at last completed, although he continued to attend the House of Lords in support of Pitt's administration. There was a growing body of opinion for seeking peace with France in view of Bonaparte's recent return there from Egypt and the introduction by Pitt of a tax on income to help pay for the war. As the century turned, Lord Cadogan was much concerned about the health of his eldest son, Charles, the last survivor of his children by Frances Bromley, whose mental faculty was becoming more enfeebled; he was 50, unmarried and undoubtedly would remain so, which meant that his eldest boy by Mary Churchill, Henry, just bought-in to a captaincy in the Life Guards, was now to all intents and purposes heir to the title and estates. Charles's condition deteriorated and on the 31st January 1800 an Inquisition held at the Thatched House Tavern in St James's Street found him to be 'a lunatic [who] doth not enjoy lucid intervals'. A committee was formed to take charge of his person and affairs, comprising Horatio Lord Walpole (Mary Churchill's brother-in-law), Hans Sloane (a great-nephew of Sir Hans Sloane and Lord Cadogan's second cousin), Colonel Charles Churchill (Mary's father) and William Dickenson, gentleman.

To the delight of Pellew, Lord St Vincent had succeeded Lord Bridport in command of the Channel fleet: 'You will have heard that we are to have a New Commander in Chief, heaven be praised. The old one is scarcely worth drowning, a more contemptible or more miserable animal does not exist.'

On January 12th the *Impetueux* sailed from Falmouth to Quiberon Bay where Pellew in concert with five other warships landed a further supply of arms for use by the Chouans, They were with the fleet again by the 12th March and on the 25th April the fleet returned to its station off Ushant where the *Impetueux* was part of a squadron detached to keep a close watch on Brest. A month later Lord St Vincent put Pellew in command of a squadron with the aim of landing a body of 4000 British troops in Quiberon Bay to stimulate the Chouan leaders into some greater action against the French government. A secondary objective was the capture of nearby Belle Ile. The troops were successfully landed on the 19th June but the officer commanding the land force, Major-General Thomas Maitland, lacked the necessary thrust to follow through, preferring to wait for reinforcements. Orders then arrived from the Secretary of State, Henry Dundas, 'the intimate friend and trusted lieutenant of Pitt', directing Maitland to send all his troops to Minorca. So Pellew then embarked the whole force and saw the transports sail on the 23rd June. Before the month was out, reinforcements arrived, too late, and the 1700 troops were landed on the island of Houat, ten miles to the north-east of Belle Ile, to await further developments. The *Impetueux* sailed for Plymouth on the 6th July but was soon heading back for Quiberon Bay to protect the British detachment encamped on Houat.

By the beginning of August a plan had been formulated by the Administration for a joint-services attack on Ferrol, as part of a general scheme for destroying the Spanish navy at its moorings, and the *Impetueux* was included in the squadron commanded by Rear-Admiral Sir John Borlase Warren in the 74-gun *Renown*, with Pellew second-in-command. The troops, which included the four battalions from Houat and 9000 men sent from Minorca, were under the command of Lieutenant-General Sir James Pulteney. The squadron and convoy of troop transports arrived off Ferrol on the 25th August; the *Impetueux* led the way in and, with no resistance

Hand-to-hand fighting

from shore, by eight o'clock in the evening the whole army was landed with twenty guns and 250 seamen to serve them. Preparations were made to land the heavy artillery and mortars the following day. In the event, the men of the *Impetueux* need not have wet their feet for by then Pulteney had decided that the town of Ferrol could only be taken with a loss of at least 2000 men – a loss his instructions did not permit him to suffer. Accordingly on the 26th August both army and cannon were re-embarked and twenty-fours later the squadron and convoy weighed anchor and headed south-west for Vigo, where they parted company; the army sailing for Egypt and the Navy to England. The expeditions to Quiberon Bay and Ferrol had proved a military shambles but, at Pellew's right-hand, George had gained valuable experience in the movement of men and munitions.

Before the squadron sailed north again for a home port, George was given command of the Admiral's Barge in a cutting-out operation against a French privateer *La Guêpe* anchored close to the Spanish batteries in Vigo Bay. The enemy vessel, carrying 18 guns and 161 men, was boarded and carried in fifteen minutes 'after a most obstinate resistance' in which twenty-five Frenchmen were killed and forty

[67]

wounded; the British sailors and marines suffered four killed and twenty wounded.

Warren's squadron reached Plymouth on the 11th October where the *Impetueux* remained under repair until early December when she sailed again for Ushant. Just before the year closed, on the 27th December, Lord Cadogan was created Earl Cadogan and Viscount Chelsea in recognition of his political services and his unwavering support of the Pitt administration. The re-creation of the family earldom must have been the source of much satisfaction for Lord Cadogan and thenceforward his daughters, no doubt to their delight, would bear the title 'Lady' with their christian and family names. The unfortunate Charles, in accordance with custom, was accorded the Viscountcy as a courtesy title. Other advancements came on New Year's Day when Pellew was appointed Colonel of Marines and Nelson was promoted Vice-Admiral and made second-in-command of the Channel fleet.

Another change in the command structure of the Channel fleet occurred in Spring 1801 when St Vincent moved to London as First Lord of the Admiralty, to be replaced by Admiral William Cornwallis who, at the prompting of St Vincent, appointed Pellew to command yet another blockading squadron, on this occasion off the French ports of L'Orient and Rochefort. The enemy showed no inclination to emerge and the task proved tedious; a number of brigs and schooners were taken, but none was worth keeping so they were scuttled and the crews sent on shore. The squadron remained at sea for eight months and was kept provisioned by victuallers from England, periodically bringing bread, pease, beef, pork and, importantly, lemon juice, which enabled the men to remain free of scurvy – a vitamin deficiency disease which had plagued earlier mariners.

As Pellew took command of his new squadron, Pitt resigned over the issue of Catholic emancipation and was succeeded by another Tory, Henry Addington, who was in favour of making peace with France. The peace faction had

The Battle of Copenhagen, 1801

grown stronger of late as, some few weeks earlier, France and Austria had signed the Peace of Luneville. On the 2nd April, a British squadron scored a notable victory over the Danish fleet at Copenhagen after Vice-Admiral Nelson had ignored the signal of his commanding admiral to break off the battle which had been fought to force Denmark out of the league of armed neutrality. Nelson was now created Viscount Nelson of the Nile and Burnham Thorpe. In reflection of these events, preliminaries of peace between Britain and France were signed at Amiens on the 1st October, although Pellew did not learn of this until three weeks later, when he immediately returned to England, sailing into Falmouth on the 1st November.[2]

It was evident to Pellew that, following a formal peace treaty, many warships including his own would be paid off and their officers beached on half-pay. This did not alarm him unduly as he had already made his plans for a seat in Parliament. Pellew was concerned, however, that his young gentlemen, who had served him so ably, should continue their careers and accordingly on the 2nd December George, rated Master's Mate for the past seven months, went on board the

[69]

32-gun *Narcissus* as midshipman. Henry Hart joined the 32-gun *Medusa* as lieutenant four months later.[3] George had been under Pellew's command for a few days short of six years and during this time he had witnessed and taken part in much action, become in a literal sense an able seaman, and grown to manhood. On the 25th January 1802, Midshipman Cadogan, dressed in his number one uniform, with his cocked hat under his arm and clutching his journals and certificates of service, attended on board the 64-gun *Monmouth* at anchor in Valetta Harbour, Malta, for his lieutenant's examination.

Navy regulations provided that no one under twenty could be a lieutenant, but at this time a birth certificate giving a convenient date was easily come by and in any event the examining board, comprising on a foreign station the three senior captains, was more concerned to test the candidate's knowledge of navigation and seamanship and to ascertain whether he had the personality required to make a lieutenant. Evident failures were rejected and in this instance patronage was to no avail. The examination for lieutenant was the most important hurdle for an aspiring officer to clear, although it was no guarantee of a commission and there were many midshipmen 'passed for lieutenant', both young and middle-aged, for whom there would be no vacancy. George passed the examination[4] and the board felt able to vouch for 'his diligence and sobriety, he can splice, knot, reef a sail, work a ship in sailing, shift his Tides, keep a Reckoning of a ship's way by Plane Sailing and Mercator, observe by Sun or Star and find the Variation of the Compass'. They also stated that 'by certification, (he) appears to be more than Twenty Years of Age', which was not the case as George was still three months short of his nineteenth birthday.

The Peace of Amiens formally concluded the recent war on the 25th March 1802 and under the terms of the treaty the French withdrew from Rome, Naples and Egypt while Britain returned all the colonial conquests she had made at the expense of France, Spain and Holland with the exception of

Trinidad (from Spain) and Ceylon (from Holland). Malta, which Britain had captured in September 1800, was to be returned to the Knights of St John. The *Impetueux* and other warships by the score were now paid off and anchored in harbours, rivers and creeks all round the coasts. George, however, did not have long to wait for his commission and on the 12th April he was appointed to a lieutenancy in the 38-gun *Leda*[5] in the Channel fleet under Captain George Hope, an event which preceded by seven weeks his sister Lady Emily's marriage to the Honourable Gerald Valerian Wellesley, a thirty-year-old cleric and a younger son of an Irish peer, the late Earl of Mornington, who had four other surviving sons. Richard, the eldest, had inherited the earldom in 1781 and had been sent to India in 1798 as Governor-General, in recognition of which he had been created Marquess Wellesley in the year following. William had acquired the fortune and name of a rich cousin and was now called Wellesley-Pole. Arthur, a career soldier, was also in India, in command of a division with the rank of major-general. Henry, the youngest son, a former soldier and member of the Irish Parliament, was Private Secretary to Richard Wellesley.

In January 1803 Lady Harriet Cavendish, a daughter of the Duke of Devonshire, writing to a friend in Paris, recorded that:

Lady Emily Wellesley has not yet made her appearance, as Gerald is so anxious that she should be admired that he will not let her stir out because he does not think her in good looks. She is not quite so protecting to his beauty, as when Mama mentioned the beauty of the Wellesley family to her one morning, the first time she ever saw her, she stopped her by exclaiming 'Oh! as for Gerald's looks, I cannot boast much of them'.[6]

Many admirers of the French scene had again crossed the Channel, including Mary Churchill who had taken up residence in the family home at Nancy. The Reverend Cooper, now succeeded to the baronetcy following the death of Sir Grey in 1801, also travelled to France.

[71]

The Marquess Wellesley

In the event, the Amiens treaty settled nothing; it was merely a breathing space during which Bonaparte took the opportunity to incorporate Piedmont into the French Republic and to intervene in the affairs of Switzerland; he also began preparing a fleet for the invasion of Britain. Faced with this threat, Britain had no alternative but to respond and in the House of Commons on the 8th March the Chancellor of the Exchequer brought down a message from the King:

His Majesty thinks it necessary to aquaint the House of Commons, that, as very considerable military preparations are carrying on in the ports of France and Holland, he has judged it expedient to adopt additional measures of precaution for the security of his dominions.

The most urgent requirement was to bring the Navy up to fighting strength and immediately work began to re-commission the laid-up warships; half-pay officers were re-called to duty and the press gangs went on patrol again. With the fleet mobilized, Britain seized the initiative and declared war on France on the 17th May 1803, bringing to an end the uncertain peace which had lasted less than twenty months.

These momentous events did not impinge too much on the thoughts of Lady Charlotte who on the 20th September and after a whirlwind romance married, following his return from India, her brother-in-law Henry Wellesley, much against the wishes of his family. Lady Wellesley had written to her husband on the 22nd August:

... You will be very surprised to hear that Henry is to be married immediately to Lady Emily Wellesley's sister, who is neither wealthy nor pretty. Poor Henry is so idle, so lazy that I am sure that it is only the fact he met this young lady in Gerald's house, where he was staying and where she was staying with her sister, that made him fall in love with her rather than her beauty or her virtue. It has been said that no Wellesley will have a fine marriage and if yours is not the best, at least you were wise enough to wait before getting engaged. Gerald and Henry would have been better advised to have done so as both their ladies are very high spirited and very gay. I have always found Lady Emily very pleasant, honest and kindly and her manners are very different to those of your wretched mother and your false and sullen sister. As for your mother, I have always compared her society to that of the Freemasons where only those sharing the secrets are accepted and where the others are novices. Your mother and sister are both furious about this wedding. As for me, I shall not take sides. I do not care for them and they do not care for me. Let them resolve the matter. The two sisters love him dearly but he was caught in their net ...[7]

Lady Wellesley wrote again on the 25th September:

... I have just received a lovely letter from Lady Emily Wellesley telling me that she had just returned from church where her dear sister was given away by Gerald and that they were all very excited. The marriage took place at Lord Cadogan's house (Downham Hall) although no other member of the family was present. The couple went to spend a week at Mr. Singleton's ...[8]

Henry's mother, the Dowager Lady Mornington, then recorded her thoughts on the matter in a letter to her eldest son, Lord Wellesley, on the following 3rd February:

The surprise, and, I must confess, vexation of dearest Henry's sudden determination to marry and form the same odious connection that Gerald had done, affected my spirits beyond all description. He also looked so dreadfully ill that I thought the first day he arrived that he really would not live many months. He is, thank God, better in health, tho' still very thin, and as he seems to be perfectly happy, I do all I can to reconcile myself to his having been taken by *storm*. I flew from them and took a long journey into Wales, and really think the air of old Bryn Kinalt, the romantick scenes in the mountains, and getting into different society and the total change gave strength both to my body and mind.

I believe Lady Charlotte is a good natured sort of person. It is impossible but she must love Henry and feel that she is in a situation infinitely beyond what she could expect, therefore I hope she will make it her study to render him happy, but I can see no charm of either person or manner, *mais il ne faut pas disputer les goûts*, and he must certainly be a better judge than I can possibly pretend to be of what constitutes his own happiness. Lady Emily, her sister, who is a second Duchess of Zorn for enterprise, etc., etc., was determined that this match should take place from the moment she heard of Henry's arrival, and laid her plans accordingly. I *can* forgive Lady Charlotte, but for *her* I confess 'tis out of my power to get over the vexation and cruel disappointment she has occasioned me.

I beg that this 'épanchement de cœur' may be 'entre nous' & I beseech you to destroy this letter.[9]

Doubts and dismay notwithstanding, the Cadogan and Wellesley families were now firmly interlocked.

CHAPTER V

First Command

As the war with France was renewed, George remained on board the *Leda*[1], now under the command of Captain Robert Honeyman who had a small squadron under his orders, stationed off the French coast near Boulogne, for the purpose of thwarting an enemy strike from the east. On the 29th September 1803 part of Honeyman's force, including the *Leda*, attacked a division of French gun-boats and drove two of them on shore. Pellew, now a member of Parliament for Barnstaple, returned to the fray as captain of the 80-gun *Tonnant*, also serving with the Channel fleet still commanded by Cornwallis; while Nelson hoisted his flag in the *Victory* as Commander-in-Chief, Mediterranean with the object of blockading a French squadron at Toulon, commanded by Rear-Admiral Louis La Touche-Tréville. Throughout the summer months and into the autumn Bonaparte continued to reinforce his Grande Armée of 120,000 men and his hand was strengthened on the 9th October when France, already allied to the Dutch, formed an alliance with Spain. Seven months later Pitt returned to 10, Downing Street and in the week following, Bonaparte was proclaimed Emperor Napoleon by the French senate.

News of these latter events did not reach George for some weeks as, at the end of March 1804, he had departed the turbulent green waters of the Channel for the generally calmer, blue waters of the Caribbean where at Port Royal, Jamaica on the 4th May he took command of the 18-gun sloop of war, *Cyane*[2], a small man-of-war reckoned below the sixth-rate. This promotion to commander, a rank awarded by selection not seniority, meant that George on the eve of his twenty-first birthday would henceforth be known and referred to as 'Captain Cadogan'. To mark his new status he wore the coveted gold epaulette on the left shoulder of his uniform coat and he was now 'one of those gilded individuals for whom bosun's mates pipe the side and who could look forward with confidence to eventual promotion to captain'[3], referred to in the Navy as 'post rank'.

The Admiralty, with regard to the difficulty of sailing eastward against the prevailing wind and current, had divided the Caribbean into two commands; the Leeward Island Station, to which George was attached, covered the eastern area, and the Jamaica Station was responsible for the western area. The commander-in-chief of the Leeward Island Station had his headquarters at Bridgetown, Barbados, while his opposite number on the Jamaica Station was based at Cape Nicolas Mole at the north-western end of Haiti. The Mole provided a good anchorage on the Windward Passage, a natural gap forty-five miles wide between San (Santo) Domingo and Cuba and one of the main exits through the island chain for ships bound for Europe. Henry Dundas (later Viscount Melville) wrote to Lord Spencer in January 1801 that '. . . It is of the utmost importance to prevent any great alarm arising on account of our West Indies interests either in Jamaica or the Leeward Islands. So much property is embarked in both these quarters, any disaster in either would produce disagreeable convulsions at home.'[4] The Navy's rôle, therefore, was to protect British merchant trade and to prevent French and Spanish merchantmen and warships operating in the islands or the Spanish Main – that stretch of coast from the Panama isthmus to the mouth of the Orinoco. Strategically, the situation was complicated by the fact that the three warring powers each had a haphazard territorial interest in the islands and San Domingo was host to all three. Every island had at least one bay or inlet from where a licenced privateer could operate, so that each of the three nations, given the availability

of ships for escort duty, had to convoy its merchantmen.

The chance of being killed by the French or Spanish, however, was slight in comparison with succumbing to the malignant yellow fever which attacked suddenly and without warning, regardless of rank. An acute headache, muscular pain, high fever and then death when 'the foam issues from the mouth; the eyes roll dreadfully; and the extremities are convulsed, being thrown out and pulled back in violent and quick alternate succession'. As George's half-brother Edward had found to his cost, a posting to the West Indies could be a death sentence. In the twelve months to April 1796, some 6500 white troops out of a total of 16,000 in the West Indies died of sickness, mostly victims of yellow fever. The Navy was by no means immune and in 1795 the 74-gun *Hannibal* lost more than two hundred men in six months. Those who survived, however, had opportunity for prize money and, given the comparatively high level of death from disease, the chances for promotion were much improved.

The *Cyane*, with her eighteen guns and disciplined crew, could fight almost any privateer afloat and with her speed and handiness she could cover a convoy more effectively than any ship of the line. On the 16th December, two days after Spain had declared war on Britain, the recently knighted Commodore Sir Samuel Hood, K.B., a younger brother of Lord Bridport and commander-in-chief at the Leeward Islands on board the *Serapis* at Barbados, wrote to William Marsden who earlier in the year had succeeded Evan Nepean as Secretary to the Admiralty:

SIR,

I have the satisfaction to send to their Lordships the copy of a letter from the Honourable Captain Cadogan, Commander of his Majesty's Sloop *Cyane*, giving an account of the capture of the *Buonaparté* Brig Privateer of 18 guns and 150 men, after a few minutes' running fight, which Captain Cadogan appears to have executed with judgment. I have the honour to be, &c.

SAMUEL HOOD.

SIR,

His Majesty's Sloop Cyane, off Antigua, 12th Nov. 1804.
I have the honour to inform you, that, on the 11th instant, at three A.M. off the Island of Mariegalante, after a short chase and running fight of thirty minutes, I had the good fortune to come up with and capture le *Buonaparté*, a very fine Privateer Brig, pierced for 22 guns, mounting 18 long French 8-pounders, and 150 Men. I am happy to add that we have received no material damage in our masts or hull, and have only a few Men hurt, occasioned by the explosion of a cartridge on the main-deck. We found the *Buonaparté* in a very shattered condition, having lost her fore-mast, bowsprit, and top-masts, in an action with three English Letters of Marque, three days previous to her capture. I should not do justice to my feelings were I to omit expressing my thorough satisfaction at the steady and determined conduct of all the officers and crew of the *Cyane*; and

although the state of the vessel was such as not to call forth any extraordinary exertions on their part, I feel confident that whenever chance may give them an opportunity, they will do ample justice to the character which in my opinion they so justly deserve. I have the honour to be, &c.

GEORGE CADOGAN.[5]

The likelihood of invasion in England appeared more threatening now that France and Holland had an openly declared belligerent ally in Spain. Napoleon's initial strategy was for the French squadrons in port at Brest, Rochefort and Toulon, the Spanish squadrons in Ferrol, Cadiz and Cartagena and the Dutch squadron at the Texel, to escape the blockading British squadrons, rendezvous in the West Indies, then as one invincible fleet to return to the Channel, annihilate the British Navy and so clear the way for his Grande Armée to invade England. Following an unsuccessful attempt, however, by the Rochefort and Toulon squadrons to unite in January 1805, Napoleon revised his plan. The new aim was for the Toulon squadron, now commanded by Vice-Admiral Pierre Villeneuve, together with the squadrons from Brest, Cadiz and Ferrol, to rendezvous at Martinique and then return eastwards to the Channel as a combined battle fleet. Villeneuve escaped the blockade at the end of March and, with Nelson in belated pursuit, met the Spanish squadron from Cadiz at Martinique. The ships from Brest and Ferrol were unable to effect their escapes and accordingly when the French admiral heard that Nelson was somewhere astern he disregarded Napoleon's orders and set sail for home. On the 22nd July, off Finisterre, the Franco-Spanish fleet was intercepted by a British squadron led by Vice-Admiral Sir Robert Calder but, after a brief engagement in misty weather, Villeneuve succeeded in bringing his fleet into Ferrol only to face a charge of cowardice by Napoleon. Nelson returned to England on the 20th August and remained until the 15th September, when he sailed on board the *Victory* for station off Cadiz.

Villeneuve's squadron had opportunity during its dash to

the Caribbean to take a number of prizes, including a convoy of British sugar-ships, and on the 12th May H.M. Sloop of War *Cyane* was forced to surrender when confronted by the overwhelming fire-power of the French frigates *Hortense* and *Hermione*. This was a sad blow for George in his first command, more particularly as only some few days earlier he had captured a Spanish privateer, the *Justicia*, which had 4 guns and ninety-five men on board. Captain Antoine Delamare de Lameillerie, in command of *Hortense*, subsequently reported to Villeneuve:

In the roads off Martinique the 15th May 1805

I am pleased to inform you that, cruising with the frigate *Hermione* in accordance with your orders at latitude 14°36' north and longitude 61°20' west, on the 11th of this month at five o'clock in the evening I saw a war ship that I judged to be the enemy from its reconnaissance signals, heading towards us under full sail. I waited for it and hoisted the English flag and he did the same immediately. I identified it as an English corvette and very shortly it was in cannon range to windward. Realising its mistake it altered course and took flight. I tacked and with a stormy gale blowing to the east chased it through the night. The enemy sailed as close to the wind as it could, tacking many times, and I followed each movement. At last, having tried by all means to escape, its cannons and some of its guns were thrown into the sea and it struck its flag without fighting. I asked its captain on board and he named himself as the Honourable George Cadogan, commander of the King's corvette *Cyane* carrying 28 cannons with a crew of 125 men, seven days out from Barbados and cruising to windwards of Martinique.

DELAMARE LAMEILLERIE[6]

On the 27th May, his ship still anchored off Martinique, he wrote to the French Minister of Maritime and Colonial Affairs:

I am pleased to report to your excellency that on the 11th May cruising 110 leagues east of Martinique, having been sent ahead of Vice-Admiral Villeneuve's squadron, I captured jointly with the

9523.
1.
26. 8bre

11,472

À Bord de *Le Bucentaure* en Rade de *Fort de France* le *27* Floréal an 13 et le *premier* du Règne de NAPOLEON.

Le Vice-Amiral **VILLENEUVE**, Grand Officier de la Légion d'honneur, Commandant en chef l'Escadre Impériale dans *les mers*, de l'Amerique.

À S.E. le ministre de la marine et des colonies.

M. Jurien
26. 8bre

Monseigneur

J'ai l'honneur d'informer S.E. de la prise de la corvette anglaise le *Cyane*, commandée par l'honorable capne Cadogan, qui a amené son pavillon aux deux frégates de S.M. l'*Hortense* et *l'Hermione*.

Le bâtiment armé de 24 bouches à feu et de 185 hommes d'équipage, croisait depuis sept jours en vent de la martinique.

Je joins ici le rapport, qui m'a fait le capne l'Ameillerie commandant *l'Hortense*.

Je prie S.E. d'agréer l'hommage de mon respect.

Villeneuve

Villeneuve's report on the capture of the Cyane

Hermione, the English corvette *Cyane* carrying 28 cannons and a crew of 125 men. Mr. Cadogan, commander of the corvette, has caused much damage to commerce in this area during the past year. He struck his flag without firing a shot.[7]

It is evident that, notwithstanding more than nine years' service, George had fallen victim to a *ruse de guerre* although, of course, he would have had no reason to suspect the presence of an enemy squadron. There was clearly some confusion or misinformation as to the number of guns *Cyane*[8] was carrying. The sloop and her complement were taken to Fort de France on Martinique where, in due course, an exchange of prisoners was arranged in time for George's appointment to another sloop of war, the 18-gun *Ferret*[9], on the 22nd March 1806.

On return to office Pitt immediately commenced negotiations for a Third Coalition and on the 9th August 1805 Austria, in return for a British subsidy of £3,000,000, joined with Britain, Russia and Sweden in a new alliance to fight France and her allies. Napoleon, recently self-proclaimed King of Italy, saw that his plans to invade England were of no avail following the Villeneuve debacle, so redeployed his Grande Armée away from the Channel coast to campaign against the other members of the Third Coalition. On the 20th October Marshal Ney inflicted a major defeat on the Austrians at Ulm, forty miles south-west of Marlborough's battlefield at Blenheim. Eleven hundred miles south-west, at Cadiz, Villeneuve's Franco-Spanish fleet had left harbour on Napoleon's express orders and against Villeneuve's better judgement, to sail to Naples to forestall any British attempt to reinforce the Austrians from the south.

The scene was set for an epic battle off Cape Trafalgar which resulted in a crushing defeat for the enemy fleet at the hands of Nelson, who died at the moment of victory. Seven thousand men, including Villeneuve, and seventeen enemy warships were captured. Two thousand six hundred French and Spanish sailors were killed or wounded while the British

Lord Nelson

sustained 1700 casualties with no loss of ships, although half were badly damaged. 'The sailing-ship of the line, the loveliest engine of warfare hammered out by the hand of man, fought at Trafalgar her last great fight'[10], and established British naval supremacy. Defeat at sea did not lessen Napoleon's territorial ambitions, however, and on the 2nd December, after occupying Vienna, he vanquished a combined Austro-Russian army at the battle of Austerlitz, forcing Austria to sue for peace once again and the Russians to retreat. The Third Coalition was shattered.

The *Ferret* operated on the Jamaica Station commanded by Rear Admiral Sir Richard Dacres and this change of location gave George opportunity, when his ship called at Port Royal for refitting, to enjoy local society and to accept the invitations to dine that could be relied upon from wealthy planters. George's great-grandmother, Lady Sloane, had been married firstly to a plantation owner in Jamaica, and no doubt this family connection resulted in a busier social round than was usual. This would act as a much needed counter-balance to his time at sea when, as captain, service tradition forced him to lead an essentially solitary existence carrying, in this subtropical zone, the additional burdens of the ever-present threat of yellow fever, unpredictable currents, and the hazards of the hurricane season.

Life for the crew also had its own particular problems as they could only very rarely be given shore-leave in the form of a 'day's liberty', due to fears of desertion. Some men had been at sea for maybe four or five years at a stretch, only setting foot on shore occasionally for expeditions to replenish the water barrels and to gather wood; their one consolation, aside from the daily issue of grog, the women that might be allowed on board when the ship lay at some convenient anchorage. The key to a reasonably content ship's crew in these harsh conditions was, again, individual self-discipline underwritten by the threat of the lash. The balance needed was a fine one; punish too little and a ship could lose its fighting edge; punish in excess and the men might mutiny, as Captain Hugh Pigot of the frigate *Hermione* found to his cost while, like George, serving on the Jamaica station. On the 20th September 1797 Pigot, 'the cruellist captain in the service', had caused three young seamen reefing the topsails during a squall, to fall to their death by threatening to 'flog the last man down'. With no hint of remorse he ordered that the 'lubbers' be thrown overboard. On the day following, he ordered a mass flogging of twelve of the remaining 'topmen'. Pigot had driven his men too far and that evening they rose in revolt and killed him and nine other officers before sailing to the Spanish port of La Guaira in Venezuela. In his previous command, the 32-gun *Success*, Pigot had logged during one thirty-eight week period, eighty-five separate floggings, or close on 1500 lashes.[11] A captain faced with a mutinous crew needed a steely character, together with some measure of good fortune, to bring the men under his control again and re-establish the vital balance. Pellew had shown the way on the *Impetueux* and as events would prove, George had learned the lesson.

The crew of the *Ferret* clearly did not take a liking to their new commander who found it necessary to threaten the fore-topmen with a flogging, 'if they did not reef the foretopsail as quick as the main'. The situation festered and led to a handful of the men determining, in an emulation of the *Hermione* mutiny, to kill George and take the ship to La Guaira. On the night of the 2nd October the first lieutenant, Mr White, was awoken in his cot by three loud cheers and a pounding of feet on the deck above, accompanied by shouts of 'Guard the Hatches!' George then appeared at the gunroom door, naked, with a pistol in one hand and a cutlass in the other – very much in the Pellew tradition – exclaiming 'Officers are you armed?' He then dashed to the after-hatchway which was blocked by a crowd of sailors, followed by White who described the un-folding course of events:

Then Captain Cadogan with his pistol pointing to the breast of Edward Jones, who was the only man I saw armed, with a cutlass in the face of his Captain, who was asking him at the same time the cause of their mutinous and dastardly conduct. The answer was 'ill-usage'. Captain Cadogan immediately disarmed the man, saying that he had but one life to lose and he would have one of them.

Faced with this steady resolve, the mutineers' courage evaporated and one by one those others who, unnoticed by White, were also armed, dropped their cutlasses and pikes. The ringleaders were put in irons and Marine Grey who had been chosen to assassinate George was asked by him the reason for the rising. 'Ill usage by flogging and starving' came the reply, to which George rejoined that he would not shoot him, 'for I am more of a gentleman'.[12] The 15th Article of War provided that 'Every person in or belonging to the Fleet, who shall desert, or entice others to do so, shall suffer death ...' and accordingly before the month was out, twelve members of the *Ferret*'s crew were hanged at Port Royal. This attempt by a crew to seize their ship and take it to the enemy was the last occasion on which it happened. Less than twelve months later the *Ferret* had a new commander and he too found the crew obdurate.

On the day that George took command of the *Ferret*, Mr Charles Grey (later Viscount Howick then the 2nd Earl Grey), First Lord of the Admiralty, put pen to paper and addressed a letter to King George III

Mr Grey humbly begs leave to submit to your Majesty the request of Admiral Villeneuve to be permitted to return, with a limited number of the officers immediately attached to him, to France. The liberal treatment of Captn Cadogan & the prisoners who fell into the hands of Admiral Villeneuve in the West Indies may perhaps induce your Majesty to approve of this indulgence being granted to Adml. Villeneuve, which the situation of your Majesty's subjects detained as prisoners in France, certainly could not have entitled him to expect.

Mr Grey having expressed to your Majesty some apprehension for the safety of the *Egyptienne*, has now the satisfaction of informing your Majesty that letters have been received this morning from Ld St Vincent, enclosing one from Captain Paget dated the 9th of March off Cape Finisterre, announcing the capture of the *Alcide*, a frigate built ship pierced for 34 guns, which was cut out of the harbour of Muros, tho' lying under the protection of two batteries, by the boats of the *Egyptienne* under the command of Captn Handfield.[13]

The King replied from Windsor Castle on the 23rd March:

The King does not object to Mr Grey's proposal that Admiral Villeneuve and a limited number of the officers immediately attached to him may be permitted to return to France. His Majesty is glad to hear that the apprehensions respecting Captain Paget are groundless.[14]

Admiral Villeneuve was duly returned to France and on his way back to Paris he stopped at Rennes to discover whether and how Napoleon would receive him. On the 23rd April he was found dead in bed with six stab wounds to the heart having, so it was said, committed suicide. Captain Charles Paget, RN, was a younger brother of Lord Paget, who before too long was to visit consternation upon the Cadogan and Wellesley families and fulfil the worst forebodings of Lady Charlotte's mother-in-law, Lady Mornington.

William Pitt died on the 23rd January 1806 at the age of 46, worn out by his patriotic exertions. Lord Grenville, a Whig, then came to office with his 'Ministry of all the Talents', which included Fox as Foreign Secretary. Napoleon's armies continued their conquering marches with only small hindrances which were swiftly overborne. He had crowned himself Emperor in 1804 and his brother Joseph was now created King of Naples; two months later another brother Louis was given the Dutch crown. Southern Italy succumbed in July and in August the Holy Roman Empire was abolished. Prussia was emboldened to declare war on the 8th October but was soon brought to heel by Napoleon, who entered Berlin less than three weeks later. Fox did not live to hear of these autumnal disasters; his health had been deteriorating for some years and he died of dropsy at the Duke of Devonshire's house in Chiswick on the 13th September and was buried in Westminster Abbey.

It was at this time that Napoleon decided upon a policy of economic warfare in an attempt to force Britain into a peace treaty. He realized that Britain's continuing ability to oppose

Charles James Fox

him was the result of her great wealth generated by foreign trade and accordingly he planned, in co-operation with his allies and the governments of countries under his control, to close all European ports to British ships and to blockade British ports. By this 'Continental System' inaugurated by the 'Berlin Decrees', British goods could not be sold and Britain would be unable to import required commodities such as

[88]

grain and timber. Additionally, it was decreed that all British subjects on French territory be imprisoned: unwelcome news for Mary Churchill and Sir William Cooper, who could not now expect to return home until the war ended.

Lord Cadogan, in his 79th year, was less inclined now to submit himself to the rigours of the nineteen-hour coach journey to London. He remained in virtual permanent residence at Downham Hall, still served by the faithful Pearce and Mrs Vaughan, where he received regular news concerning his children. There was scant hope of Lord Chelsea's recovery. Henry was now a lieutenant-colonel in the 18th Foot, while 17 year-old Edward had just been purchased an ensign's commission in the 20th Foot. George, of course, was in the West Indies, but there was a possibility he would return next year. Lady Louisa remained at home; she was 19 and as yet showed no inclination to marriage. Both Lady Charlotte and Lady Emily had each presented their father with two grandchildren. Lady Charlotte had two sons, Henry Richard and William Henry George; while Lady Emily, now living at Chelsea where her husband had recently been appointed Rector, had a son Arthur Richard, named after her Wellesley brothers-in-law, and a daughter, Emily Anne Charlotte. As Christmas and New Year passed, Lord Cadogan must have experienced a sense of contentment. Aside from Lord Chelsea, who in any event was removed from worldly cares, all was well with the family.

CHAPTER VI

Post Rank

Lord Cadogan, 'a nobleman possessed of much urbanity', died at Downham Hall on Sunday the 5th April 1807. His last will and testament signed six years earlier expressed a 'desire to be buried privately in the Sloane Vault at Chelsea' (Old Church), but in a later codicil he gave amended and very detailed instructions as to his interment:

I now request to be Interred in the most private manner possible in the parish church of Santon Downham [St Mary's] in the County of Suffolk and laid in the South-West corner of a New Vault I have erected there which I shall in future consider as my Family Vault. I would have no Hearse or Mourning Coach attend my Funeral nor above one Undertaker's Man just to put it in proper train and would be carried from my House here to the Church by Ten of the Labourers (Parishioners if possible) among which may be included my two Garden Men, Carpenter and Warrener, who shall have two Guineas each and a good clock Hat and Hat band for so doing but no Eating or Drinking.

    N.B. If I should chance to die from home a hearse and four will of course be necessary to bring my remains and deposit them in my house here to be taken to interment afterwards as above directed. I would have a Monument according or nearly so to a design settled with Mr. Robert Snare Stone Mason at Thetford put up for me at the West end (of the) Church just over the vault in the place I settled with him and another to answer ready to (be) put up on the other side of the large 6'0" thick Doorway from the Church into the Belfry for my Eldest Son Lord Viscount Chelsea when he dies the inscriptions on such Monuments to be only the time of the birth and death of the party remembered and the years of their age and the same inscriptions to be put on the respective Coffin Plate which

Coffins (especially the lower one) should be of remarkable strength and thickness.[1]

Lord Cadogan's various freehold estates, aside from his Chelsea moiety which had been settled upon Lord Chelsea, were devised to Horace Lord Walpole, Hans Sloane and Joseph White, a barrister, 'To the use of or in Trust for' firstly, Henry and his male heir 'Lawfully to be begotten' then, in the event of his death without a legitimate son, to George or his son, yet to be born. In the event of George's death without lawful male heir the estates would pass to Edward on the same basis, with a remainder to the three sisters. The leasehold properties, including Cadogan House in Whitehall, were to be sold and the proceeds added to the personal estate which was to provide annual allowances for the three younger sons. Henry and George, both now having achieved their majorities, would receive £700 and £400 a year respectively, while Edward would receive £100 annually until he was twenty-one, increasing then to £300 a year. As and when one of them might succeed to the earldom, the allowance would cease. Additionally, Henry, George and Edward could each look forward to a capital sum under their mother's marriage settlement.

Lady Emily and Lady Charlotte had already received £5000 each upon the occasion of their respective marriages and Lady Louisa would have the interest on a like sum until such time as she married when she also would receive £5000. Lady Louisa was also to receive Lord Cadogan's 'Yellow Chariot' and his 'Sedan Chair'. On account of their 'long and faithful services' Joseph Pearce was left £200 and an annuity of £20 while Mrs. Vaughan was bequeathed £100 and an annuity of £10. The annuity that was earlier envisaged for Mrs Farley Bull was annulled. It is evident from the Will that Edward was originally destined for the church and one final codicil deals with his future: the executors are empowered to purchase 'further different promotions in the army till he is become a Lieutenant

Colonel in the line Service and at the then Regimental prices but not to enter into the Foot Guards on any account whatsoever.' Lord Cadogan's reluctance on this point appears to stem from Sir William Cooper's regimental allegiance. Lord Chelsea now became the 2nd Earl Cadogan of the new creation and in his will Lord Cadogan expressed the hope that the trustees would be able to arrange for him to reside at Downham Hall.

In retaliation for the Berlin Decrees, Britain had promulgated an Order in Council making neutral nations liable to confiscation of their ships and cargoes if they traded between ports from which British ships were excluded and, as the year progressed, both Britain and France endeavoured to tighten the economic screw to their own advantage. British trade suffered, causing unemployment and a rise in the price of bread, but eventually France and her allies discovered that on balance their economic loss was the greater and the Continental System was relaxed to the point of allowing French farmers to export their corn to Britain. During the week preceding Lord Cadogan's death, the King dismissed Lord Grenville as a result of his support for Catholic emancipation and on a rising tide of Tory popularity, due to their firm stance against the French and Napoleon, the Duke of Portland was returned to office; the Whigs were now destined to remain out of government until 1830. Arthur Wellesley, who had also returned from India and was now a Knight of the Bath and Member of Parliament for Rye in Sussex, joined the new administration as Chief Secretary of Ireland, while Henry Wellesley had been appointed a Secretary of the Treasury. Following a further defeat inflicted upon her by Napoleon, Russia signed the Treaty of Tilsit with France in July which included a provision for Tsar Alexander to attempt to mediate between France and Britain. By virtue of a collateral treaty he agreed, in the event of Britain refusing to come to terms, to support Napoleon and to force Denmark, Sweden and Portugal to make war on Britain. To forestall Denmark's entry into the war a British fleet bombarded Copenhagen in early September and forced the surrender of the Danish fleet.

As the Treaty of Tilsit was signed, Henry Cadogan was held prisoner of war in Spanish America. In March 1805, a British military expedition had been sent under the command of Lieutenant-General Sir David Baird to take Cape Colony in South Africa from the Dutch in order to forestall its capture by the French. Baird's mission was successful and he defeated the Dutch at the battle of Blueberg. The naval commander-in-chief Commodore Sir Hume Popham, 'a restless and ambitious man', then persuaded Baird to 'lend him a brigade' commanded by Major-General William Beresford, to take across the South Atlantic and attempt the capture of the important city of Buenos Aires which contained the Argentine Treasury. Beresford duly landed with his troops in June 1806 at the mouth of the River Plate and, having overcome Spanish resistance, captured the city and 'received as prize' the sum of 1,086,208 dollars which were sent back to England in George's former ship the *Narcissus*[2], to be gratefully received by the Treasury. Before reinforcements for Beresford were available, the local population, 'ashamed of being conquered by so few soldiers', rose against the invaders early in July 1807. Defeat for the comparatively small and isolated British force was inevitable; Beresford's left wing had already succumbed when

On the extreme right, the Forty-fifth advanced in two columns, the right under Colonel Guard, the left under Major Nichols, upon the Residencia, which had been prescribed by word of mouth as the object of its attack. This was evidently a verbal variation from the written orders; and the result was that the Forty-fifth moved by two streets a long way to south of those originally assigned to them. The place was reached, taken, and occupied with trifling loss within an hour; and thus a very strong position on the south-eastern flank of the city was secured, assuring easy communication with the fleet. Some distance to the left of Nichols, the Light Brigade moved off in two columns; the left column consisting of four companies of the

Ninety-fifth and five light companies – in all about six hundred bayonets – under the independent command of Colonel Pack; the right column of four more companies of the Ninety-fifth and four light companies, under the personal direction of [General] Craufurd. Both columns passed through the town to the beach unmolested except by a few cannon-shot from the Great Square; and Craufurd, finding the fort to be within five hundred yards of him, determined to advance upon it by the beach, sending orders to Guard to follow him with the Forty-fifth in support. No intimation, it must be observed, had been given to Craufurd that Guard was to occupy the Residencia, nor had any hint of this intention appeared in general orders.

Meanwhile Pack, having divided his column into two and given the command of half of it to Colonel Cadogan, turned northward, along two parallel streets, two blocks apart, conceiving, as had Craufurd, that the Great Square and the fort were the points where he was intended to attack. This movement brought him near the Franciscan Church, where in a moment half of his men were struck down, and he himself was wounded by the fire of an invisible enemy. Hastily retreating to the street along which he had originally advanced, he found Cadogan's party also retiring, having suffered the like maltreatment. Cadogan had led his men with little loss to the gateway of the Jesuits' College, when every man of his leading company and every horse and man attached to his single field-gun had been in an instant shot down. About half of his men had followed him into one house; the rest had dispersed themselves to seek shelter wherever they could find an open door. Cadogan himself was in great distress, declaring that he and his men had done their duty, but that success was impossible.

Profoundly impressed with the hopelessness of the enterprise, Pack made known to Cadogan his intention of withdrawing to the Residencia. Cadogan deprecated this idea; and Pack agreed to stay where he was until he should see Craufurd. That General soon appeared at the back of the Convent of St Domingo, and was presently joined by Guard, who had come with his grenadier-company from the Residencia to open communication with the Light Brigade. Pack urged upon Craufurd the impracticability of the task entrusted to him, and pressed him strongly to retire to the Residencia. Craufurd hesitated, representing the expediency of occupying the Convent of St Domingo; and Pack reluctantly gave way. The door of the convent was blown open by the second field-gun attached to the Light Brigade; the building was occupied; and the captured colours of the Seventy-first, being found within, were hoisted above it. No sooner did the British troops appear on the roof than a considerable fire was opened upon them from the adjoining houses; but there was no reason for anxiety until noon, when a Spanish officer appeared with a flag of truce. Not doubting but that the messenger bore a proposal from [General] Liniers [the Spanish commander] to capitulate, Craufurd was staggered when he was met on the contrary by the news that the Eighty-eighth had surrendered, and that Liniers called upon him also to surrender. Craufurd dismissed the flag at once with a curt refusal; but, shortly afterwards, a large body of the enemy marched into the street by the entrance to the convent and prepared to seize the field-gun, which, being too wide to be brought into the building, had been left outside. Then realising how critical was his position, Craufurd hauled down the colours which he had hoisted, and made ready to retire to the Residencia. Guard with his grenadier-company made a rush at the gun, and swept away the hostile column which threatened it; but in three minutes forty of his men were killed or wounded by the fire from the adjacent houses; and Craufurd, seeing that the evacuation of the convent was impossible, ordered the men back to their posts and resumed the defence. Presently all firing ceased except in his own immediate neighbourhood, which sign he interpreted to mean that the attack had failed at all points; and at half past three, judging that assistance or relief was hopeless, he surrendered. Cadogan, having lost ninety-seven men out of one hundred and forty, besides five officers, had surrendered some time before.[3]

The British lost more than half of their engaged force: 400 officers and men killed, 650 wounded and nearly 2000 taken prisoner – including Henry. On the 7th July, a timely suspension of hostilities was proclaimed and an agreement signed providing for an immediate release of those captured on the understanding that the British would withdraw from the Argentine within ten days. Henry's incarceration had proved of short duration.

George achieved post rank two weeks before his father's death, following his own return from the West Indies, and on the 6th October, when he was twenty-four, he read his commission on board the sixth-rate, 22-gun *Crocodile*[4] at Spithead. The promotion to post rank, signified by the transfer of the gold epaulette to the right shoulder, was the critical turning point in a naval officer's career. In reaching it he was assured that, if he lived long enough and assuming that he had not hoisted his flag earlier on merit, he was bound to become an admiral by the process of gradually obtaining a higher placing in the Navy list of captains, as those with seniority were promoted or died. When an officer reached the top of the list he was made a rear-admiral in the next set of promotions, as a vacancy occurred, changing over to the bottom of the rear-admirals' list and beginning the slow ascent through the three stages of rear-admiral, three stages of vice-admiral and two of admiral; going ashore on half-pay did not affect the process. The *Crocodile* sailed on the 15th December for a round cruise to the Cape of Good Hope, the headland of South Africa, returning to home port on the 9th May 1808. It was a dismal voyage during which there were generally two floggings each week.

Two days before the *Crocodile* anchored, the Spanish King Charles IV was forced to abdicate by Napoleon in the eventual favour of the King of Naples, Joseph Bonaparte. Napoleon realised that to make himself master of western Europe, he had to control the whole of the Iberian Peninsula encompassing both Spain and Portugal. Spain was his ally but Portugal remained on friendly terms with Britain, allowing her ships to breach the Continental System. On the 27th October 1807, therefore, France and Spain had signed the secret Treaty of Fontainebleau which allowed French troops to pass through Spain to Portugal with a view to partitioning that country between the two signatories. At the end of November 1807 a French army under General Junot entered Portugal and occupied the capital, Lisbon. During the month following,

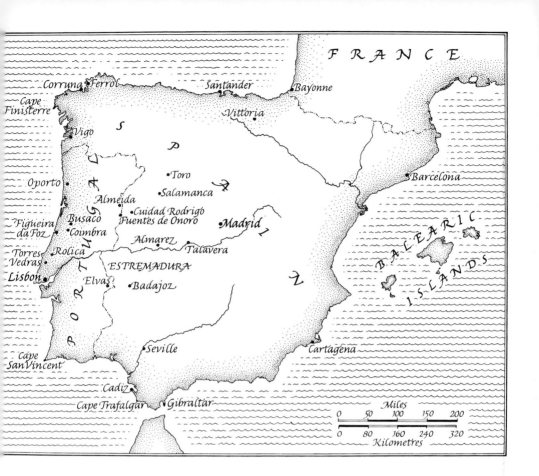

Napoleonic forces proceeded to invade Spain in defiance of the
treaty, as a prelude to seizing the Spanish throne. The Spanish
people, followed closely by the Portuguese, revolted against
the invader and, during the early weeks of summer 1808,
deputations from both countries travelled to England urging
the British government to joint action against the French. As
chance would have it, Sir Arthur Wellesley, recently promoted lieutenant-general, was in Ireland at this time in command of 9000 men preparing to embark for an invasion of
Spanish America. He was now ordered to take his force to
Portugal to create a diversion to assist the Spanish guerillas
and to expel Junot's army. Wellesley sailed from Cork on the
12th July, one day ahead of the troop transports, taking with
him as an aide-de-camp, Henry Cadogan, who had recently

[97]

transferred to the 71st Highlanders. The Peninsular War had begun.

Wellesley was keen to reach his destination as quickly as possible and accordingly, one day out from Cork, he transferred with his staff to George's fast cruiser *Crocodile*, giving the two brothers an unusual opportunity to discuss the war, their respective careers and other family matters. Their mother was lost in France; Edward earlier in the year had become a lieutenant; Lady Emily was expecting her fourth child; Lady Charlotte was also pregnant and letters-patent had been granted to Uncle Horatio Walpole and Hans Sloane for the continued custody of the new Lord Cadogan and administration of his affairs. Grandfather Churchill, now in his mid-eighties, had decided to step down from the earlier 'committee'.

The *Crocodile* reached Oporto on the 24th July and Wellesley went ashore to put in hand arrangements for food and transport for the coming campaign. He then returned on board and George set sail for a rendezvous off Lisbon to enable Wellesley to confer with Admiral Sir Charles Cotton, Commander-in-Chief, Tagus, which resulted in a decision to land the army at Montego Bay, ninety-five miles south of Oporto. The *Crocodile* then sailed north, arriving off Figueira da Foz on the 30th July. The landings began two days later and were completed within the week, at which point Wellesley's force was augmented by the arrival from Gibraltar of 5000 troops under General Sir Brent Spencer. The enlarged army began its march to Lisbon on the 9th August and a week later Wellesley encountered part of Junot's army sent from the capital to meet him, and soundly beat it at Roliça. Further reinforcements then joined him from England, bringing the strength of his force to about 17,000 men, while a further 10,000 men under Lieutenant-General Sir John Moore had arrived off the Spanish Galician coast to the north.

A difficult situation had been developing for some while over the position of commander-in-chief held by Wellesley, whose name was low in the army list of lieutenant-generals.

Post Rank

The Administration had nominated Wellesley, a Minister in the Government, while army chiefs at Horse Guards believed that Moore should be appointed. A compromise was reached and a very elderly general, Sir Hew Dalrymple, was recalled from retirement and sent to take over from Wellesley who just had sufficient time before returning to England to defeat Junot at the battle of Vimeiro on the 21st August. Dalrymple's tenure was short and unsuccessful and he was soon replaced by Moore, who had orders to march north towards Corunna on the Spanish coast to join up with a large secondary force on its way from England under Sir David Baird. With an army then of nearly 40,000 men, Moore would assist the Spanish government in driving the French forces from Spain.

Moore advanced as far as Salamanca where he was enthusiastically received but, because of lack of money and discouraging reports about the morale of his Spanish allies, he planned to return to Portugal. After desperate pleas for aid from the Spanish government in Madrid, however, he decided to advance northward against the French army commanded by Marshal Soult, positioned on the Carrion River.

Landing at Mondego Bay

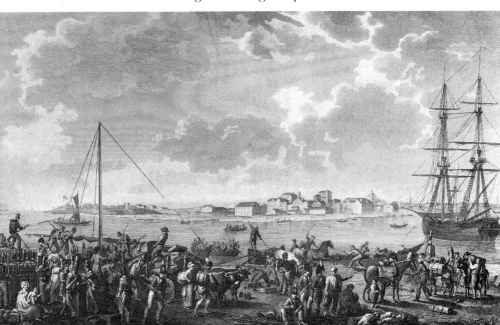

Here, learning from an intercepted message that Madrid had already fallen and that Napoleon's army had cut off his line of retreat into Portugal, he realized that to save his troops he must retire as quickly as possible to Corunna, inflicting as much damage as possible to the enemy on the way. In the meantime Baird's army had reached Spain and after some vicissitude had marched south. The two forces met on the 20th December. Moore immediately redistributed his new army and Lieutenant-General Lord Paget, who had arrived with Baird, was given command of the cavalry which, on the following day, put Soult's cavalry to flight in what was 'perhaps the most brilliant exploit of the British cavalry during the whole six years of war'.[5] Moore, preparing for the main attack on Soult, then received news that Napoleon was marching to his marshal's relief and accordingly on Christmas eve he continued his epic retreat to Corunna where he arrived on the 13th January 1809, three days ahead of the pursuing French army. A fierce action ensued in which the French were driven back and Moore was killed. Lord Paget, suffering from temporary blindness, had embarked from Corunna some few days earlier, landing in England on the 20th January.

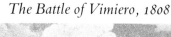

The Battle of Vimiero, 1808

CHAPTER VII

Elopement and a Duel

Henry Lord Paget, forty years old and with the reputation of a dandy, was every inch the handsome, dashing cavalry officer. He was heir to the Earl of Uxbridge and married to the beautiful Lady Caroline Villiers, younger daughter of the Earl of Jersey. They had eight children – the eldest Caroline was twelve and the youngest, Arthur, was three – and everything, apparently, augured well for the happy continuation of the marriage. Then early in 1808, while attending one of his father's musical parties at Uxbridge House in Old Burlington Street, he met and soon fell deeply in love with Lady Charlotte. She had given birth to a daughter, Charlotte Arbuthnot, in January and was there with her sisters Lady Emily and Lady Louisa. The Cadogan and Paget families had been close friends for many years. Lady Charlotte, known to everyone simply as 'Char', then twenty-six with two young sons in addition to the newly arrived baby Charlotte, responded and with the emergence of Spring they became lovers. Char had been recommended to ride regularly for the sake of her health and as Henry Wellesley was often engaged at the Treasury, Paget had taken upon himself, most willingly, the rôle of equestrian escort. Sir Arthur Wellesley later wrote that:

Lady Charlotte being considerably advanced in her pregnancy the riding parties ceased; & about this time Mr Wellesley had perceived the extraordinary attention paid to Lady Charlotte by Lord Paget, & had in consequence remonstrated with her upon the subject. Towards the close of the Session of Parliament of 1808 [in July] Mr Wellesley removed to Putney Heath [from Berkeley Square] & from that time till the return of Lady Charlotte to London in the Month

Lord Paget

Lady Paget, subsequently Duchess of Argyll

of February 1809, Mr Wellesley had every reason to believe that no meeting took place between Lady Charlotte & Lord Paget.[1]

Char gave birth to another son in the autumn of 1808; he was christened Gerald after his uncle and in early February of the following year she moved back to the more fashionable Curzon Street, off Park Lane. Char determined 'not to go out this year' to avoid arousing untoward gossip. As for Paget, she informed Henry, 'I regard him as a common acquaintance and I believe he liked my society last year but I have no reason to believe that he thinks of me in any way that can be objectionable.'[2] Henry suggested that Char should continue to enjoy the social entertainments that London had to offer but not to undertake any more riding-parties. Paget by now, however, had returned from Spain and the two lovers found their mutual attraction to be undiminished. The equestrian outings were replaced by tête-à-tête walks in Green Park, avoiding the attentions of the Wellesley footman. Paget wrote to his brother Charles:

Divest yourself of prejudice and enquire about her, and you will find that she is one of the most amiable and agreeable women in Society – devoid of all affectation, uncommonly modest, perfectly virtuous, exemplary in her conduct towards her family, truly but not ostentatiously religious, uncommonly beloved by all who know her well. Of high rank and married into a family of high rank. An attachment is unfortunately formed between us. It is fought against for a long time. Alas, not long enough – passion gets the better of reason and finally we are driven to the necessity of the present step.[3]

Charles would need some convincing for he had written to their brother Arthur: 'Oh! That that nefarious damned Hellhound should have so entrapped that before noble fine creature.'[4]

The 'present step' mentioned by Paget, referred to Char's desertion of hearth and family and their elopement. Henry Wellesley, suffering from a bout of ill-health, had noticed that, with Char, 'there was not that appearance of affectionate kindness which he had observed upon former similar occasions', and on putting the point to her, passions rose and Char left the room to the accompaniment of Henry's demand that one of them should leave the house the following day. Char was not to let this opportunity slip and the next day, having left the house ostensibly for a walk in Green Park, she dismissed the footman and stepped into a hired hackney-coach. At some little time later, on the same day, Lord Paget wrote to Arthur Paget:

At the very instant that your letter arrived, I received a message from a person in a Hackney Coach in Park Lane to come immediately.

An *Eclat* took place last night and Lady Charlotte Wellesley, dreading a further discussion this morning, that event which we have long dreaded, has actually taken place. I pity you all. Pity us in return – we are in want of it.[5]

Paget and Char availed themselves temporarily of the Mount Street lodgings of Baron Tuyll, an old friend and aide-de-camp to Paget, and Henry was able to have a letter delivered here offering to take back his erring wife. She replied by writing to Henry's friend Charles Arbuthnot who was fully aware of the elopement:

It would be the Height of Ingratitude were I not to try to convey my thanks to Henry for his most kind and generous offer of taking home a Wretch who has so injured him. I dare not write to himself but I implore it of you to say everything which Gratitude and Feeling can suggest to express my Sense of the Kindness of his Conduct. His note was forwarded to me this Morning – but degraded and unprincipled as I must appear in the eyes of everybody, believe me I am not lost to all Sense of Honor which would forbid my returning to a husband I have quitted, to children I have abandoned. Indeed, indeed, my Dear Mr Arbuthnot, if you knew all you would pity more than blame me. Could you tell all the resistance that has been made to this most criminal most atrocious attachment, could you know what are my Sufferings at this Moment you would feel for me. Henry has not deserved this of me. We have had some differ-

[105]

ences and he may perhaps have sometimes been a *little* too hard to me, but I can with truth assert & I wish you to publish it to the World that in essentials and indeed in trifling subjects, he has ever been *kind to me to the greatest Degree*. Nor has the Person (who may be supposed to have attempted to lower him in my estimation in order to gain my affections) ever spoken of him to me but in the Highest Terms of Respect. About my dear dear children I must say one word. Do you think I dare hope ever by any remote or indirect means to hear sometimes of them? You know how much I love them, you are aware of their merits and what I must feel at having quitted them but I have the satisfaction, the inexpressible comfort of knowing they will be taken care of by their Father though their Mother has abandoned them. My dear little Henry and Charlotte, God bless you.

It is perhaps significant that no mention is made of baby Gerald.[6]

On the 8th March Paget's father addressed a heartrending appeal to Char:

DEAR MADAM,

Let me on my knees implore you to listen to the prayer of an aged & perhaps dying Father, and to restore my Son to his distracted Family, which for ever will render me your Grateful & Faithful Servant,

UXBRIDGE[7]

Char was unyielding and Lord Uxbridge, in deep depression, threatened to cut off his son without a farthing. Other members of the Paget family were equally incensed and Paget's brother Charles wrote: 'my God, how dreadful, and all this unbounded misery and disgrace and for the most wicked and profligate whore and liar that ever hell itself could or ever will produce.' Sir Arthur Wellesley was in no doubt as to what had happened: 'Paget appears to have gone mad', he wrote to the Duke of Richmond on the 10th March. 'He has written a letter to his father which bears evident symptoms of derangement . . .'[8]

The general atmosphere was becoming ever more charged

and Paget and Char went into hiding as their affair was now the subject of newspaper interest and the talk of the town. Lady Harriet Cavendish wrote to her brother, the Marquis of Hartington, on the 8th March:

I dined at Devonshire House yesterday and found it cold and dismal; London is full of impenetrable fog and horror at Lord Paget's elopement – he went off the day before yesterday with Lady Charlotte Wellesley. It is in every way shocking and unaccountable. He has left his beautiful wife and 8 or 9 children and she a husband whom she married about 5 years ago, for love, and who is quite a Héro de Romance in person and manner, with 4 poor little children. He left a letter for Lord Uxbridge saying that he had a great esteem and affection for Lady Paget but could not resist taking the step he had done. I have heard nothing of her or indeed any particulars but those I have told you. Pray, dearest Hartington, marry somebody you will like to stay with. I believe Lady Paget is a very great fool though do not imagine that I mean that or anything as an excuse for him – I think him inexcusable and detestable.

How the White Hart will ring with my aunt Spencer's comments upon this event and how dearest Douaire Zara and Sarah will mourn over the world and its enormities. They can none of them say or feel too much, yet the miserable destiny Lady C. Wellesley has prepared for herself will bring its own punishment and it is impossible not to feel the greatest compassion for her.[9]

Lady Harriet wrote again on the following day:

Just after I sent my letter yesterday Farquhar arrived from Uxbridge House. He had seen the letter Lord Paget had left with his father. It was to say that he was as well aware as any body could be of the villainy of his conduct and the ruin and infamy it would bring upon himself – that he had the greatest esteem and affection for his wife and adored his children, but that he had long been irresistibly attached to Lady Charlotte. He had begged for foreign service, exposed himself in every way (which, by the bye, every body says was really the case – that no commanding officer ever put himself so forward in danger), hoping from day to day to die in the bed of honour – that when he returned from Spain he was unfortunately thrown again into her society and though his eyes were open to all the dreadful consequences, he could not resist doing what he had done – and having ruined her, thought himself in honour bound to ruin himself also – that he should now go with her to some Island in the Archipelago where he might never be heard of more, only begging that any spark of regard that his family and friends might have felt for him should be all turned to the consolation and welfare of his wife and children.

Sir Walter also saw Lady Charlotte's letter to her friends, which was to say that no human being ever would hear of her again as she should in future live only to the man who was willing to sacrifice everything for her sake. Sir Walter knew her and talked of her with abhorrence – she has left her husband in a very dangerous state of health and 4 poor little deserted children. Henry Wellesley made some discovery the day before she went off – very high words passed between them and he told her that either she or him must leave the house. The next morning, before any body was up, she walked out into the Green Park – where she met Mr. Arbuthnot – he spoke to her and she only begged him not to delay her, that she was going to take a step she should probably repent to the latest hour of her life. Her manner was so hurried and extraordinary that he was convinced she said this to get rid of him and that she was going to drown herself and watched her till she had passed the water. She got into a Hackney coach and drove to Ld Paget's home, from whence they eloped. There are many reports this morn^g – some people say they are still in Town, that his family have got at him and are trying to persuade him not to leave England, others that Henry Wellesley and him fought yesterday and that Lord Paget was killed – I shall probably know the truth before I send my letter. It is a dreadful tragedy all together and the horror and consternation at it is what it ought to be – deeply and generally felt. She has very little beauty but I believe her powers of pleasing to have been uncommonly great and her Coquetry unfortunately in proportion. It is an awful lesson and a warning to women; what must her feelings be if she has any. There can be nothing so terrible as to bring misery upon a man really attached to one – it would be better a thousand times to die oneself and think only of what she occasions to Lord Paget, and probably the last act of this eventful history is yet to come.

There has been no Duel. God bless you, dearest brother.[10]

Lord Hartington received a final communication on the matter dated the 16th March:

Lord Paget is alive – the report of the Duel was false, but many of his friends say that he is in so distracted a state that they should not at any time be surprised to hear of his having destroyed himself. He said to his Aide de camp the morning he was leaving his home to join Lady Charlotte, 'The best thing you could do for me would be to run your sword through my body.' He seems to have acted as much upon a false idea of honour as from the force of passion. He believed himself to share the ruin he had brought upon her and forgets in this desperate and fallacious reasoning the sacred claims that a wife and children have upon him and how absurd it is to talk of honour at the moment of abandoning them.

Lady Paget is in great distress but I fancy his conduct to her has for a long time been inexcusable. He has written to Lord Uxbridge to say that hers has always been irreproachable and that her encouragement of Sir Arthur and Lady Boringdon, for which she has been so much blamed, was in obedience to his express command. You should hear Miss Berry upon the subject – 'oh it is a pretty story, a very pretty story. Lady Charlotte leaves 4 children, the youngest four months old and just weaned, oh, but it is a pretty story. Lord Paget devotes himself to ruin and disgrace and for what a strapping lass I would hardly hire for my kitchen maid – oh, but it is the very prettiest story.' And so she goes on crescendo with anger – *the*'s and *but*'s till entire loss of breath forces her to stop.[11]

Char's brothers, suffering an amalgam of embarrassment, concern and annoyance, decided to intervene and Baron Tuyll was given a letter for her signed jointly by them, requiring that she should at once give Paget up and threatening, in the event of her refusing, to call him out. Paget's brother-in-law, Lord Enniskillen, felt that the Cadogan brothers were:

most violent. They *will* have her or the most fatal consequences may be the result. The elder brother offers her his entire protection. I trust the fear of losing her last resources and the dread of Paget's life (as the lewdness is now pretty well over it is supposed) may work upon her – It is our last shift & if this does not do, Paget must be lost for ever.[12]

[109]

Eight days after the elopement the Duke of Sussex, a younger son of George III, informed Lord Graves, another brother-in-law to Paget, that according to his personal surgeon, Char's brother Colonel Cadogan had 'just arrived, attended by a friend, Expres to call out Paget'. Henry's second had earlier visited the Duke's surgeon to put him on notice that 'you will be ready to attend me at any time in the course of the day – or when I send for you'. Graves reported, 'that d–d meddling Duke threatened to give the information at Bow Street for the apprehension of the Parties', and Graves had respectfully to suggest that such interference in a matter so delicate would be highly improper and indecorous. Charles Paget, on being advised of the development, had no intention of stopping any duel for 'it might by some miracle dissolve the cursed connection as it now exists'. There was no immediate development, however, and Graves told Arthur Paget that: 'both Mr H. Wellesley and Cadogan vote that stinking Pole Cat not worth the shedding blood. Damn her! How Paget's stomach will heave in the course of six months, when she seizes him in her hot libidinous arms.'[13]

Henry Cadogan then made an attempt to find some less potentially violent solution to the problem, and he sent a message to Char that if she would give up Paget he would 'sell out of the Army in order entirely to devote himself to her protection'. Char, however, was 'inexorable and will not even consent to seeing her Brother. Paget at the same time says that he will not attend to any Challenges from anybody, but that if Henry Wellesley or the Cadogans feel themselves aggrieved they may come to his lodgings and shoot him.' Calmer counsels then prevailed and the two lovers were persuaded to part for a month to allow time for passions to cool. Enniskillen was moved to reflect: 'Now, every Engine should be at work to put a final stop to it, for how long this separation will be I know not. I wish I could get some huge Paddy to satisfy her lust and outdo Paget.'[14] The separation, however, was short-lived and Charles Paget recorded: 'They are now actually

Henry Cadogan

together again, but their plans are not settled whether to continue in or leave town. If they do the latter, we have still to see what the Cadogans are made of.'[15]

Henry, effectively the head of his family, rose to the occasion and penned a letter to Lord Paget:

March 28, 1809

I hereby request you to name a time and place where I may meet you, to obtain satisfaction for the injury done myself and my whole family by your conduct to my sister.

I have to add that the time must be as early as possible, and the place not in the immediate neighbourhood of London, as it is by concealment alone that I am able to evade the Police.[16]

To which Paget replied:

I have nothing to say in justification of my conduct towards your sister, but that it has been produced by an attachment perfectly unconquerable. She has lost the world upon my account, and the only atonement I can make is to devote myself, not to her happiness (which with her feeling mind is, under the circumstances, impossible) but to endeavour, by every means in my power to alleviate her suffering. I feel, therefore, that my life is hers, not my own. It distresses me beyond description to refuse you that satisfaction which I am most ready to admit you have the right to demand: but upon the most mature reflection, I have determined upon the propriety of this line of conduct.

My cause is bad indeed: but my motive for acting thus is good: nor was I without hopes that you would have made allowances for this my very particular situation, and thereby have largely added to the extreme kindness you have already shewn to your sister upon this afflicting occasion.[17]

Henry passed this response to his proposed second 'Mr. Sloane', together with a request that he show the correspondence to any of his friends who might wish to read it 'in order that what has passed may not be misrepresented'. He continued to Sloane:

It is not unknown to you that I have by concealment alone been able for some time to evade the Police, who having anticipated the step I was likely to take, are continuing in pursuit of me. Under these circumstances it would ill become me to apply to the conduct of Lord Paget the expressions that my feelings at this moment dictate: and I shall therefore leave it to you and others to determine whether the line he has thought proper to adopt on this occasion is or is not the most honourable.[18]

Henry was now exasperated with the whole business; Paget would not fight him and his sister would not pay him heed. Accordingly, he went to see Sir Arthur Wellesley who had recently resigned from the Cabinet, and obtained permission to accompany him on his imminent return to Portugal.

George was not, however, inclined to let the matter rest and following Henry's departure with Wellesley on the 14th April, he issued two challenges, the second one of which was accepted, probably because Paget now felt satisfied that in the event of his death Char and her children would be cared for.

Elopement and a Duel

The duellists and their seconds, Captain M'Kenzie of the Royal Navy for George and Lieutenant-Colonel Hussey Vivian for Paget, met on Wimbledon Common at seven o'clock on the morning of the 30th May. The chosen weapons were pistols and the adversaries, twelve paces between them, were instructed to fire simultaneously.

Captain Cadogan fired, Lord Paget's pistol flashed – this having been decided to go for a fire, a question arose whether Lord Paget had taken aim as intending to hit his antagonist. Both the seconds being clearly of opinion that such was not his intention (although the degree of obliquity he gave the direction of the pistol was such as to have been discovered only by particular observation), Captain M'Kenzie stated to Capt. Cadogan that as it appeared to be Lord Paget's intention not to fire at him, he could not admit of the affair proceeding any further. Lt. Col. Vivian then asked Capt. Cadogan whether he had not observed himself that Lord Paget had not aimed at him? To which he replied in the affirmative. Capt. M'Kenzie then declared his determination not to remain any longer in the field, to witness any further act of hostility on the part of Capt. Cadogan. Capt. C. replied, of course his conduct must be decided by his second; declaring at the same time that he had come prepared for the fall of one of the parties. On Capt. M'Kenzie and Lt. Col. Vivian making it known to Lord Paget that as he evidently did not intend to fire at Capt. Cadogan, the affair could go no further, Lord P. replied: 'As such is your determination, I have no hesitation in saying that nothing could ever have induced me to add to the injuries I have already done to the family by firing at the brother of Lady Charlotte Wellesley.' The parties then left the ground.[19]

Paget was also under attack from Henry Wellesley, who had issued proceedings against him for criminal conversation and the action was heard before a jury in the Sheriff's Court on the 12th May. Wellesley won his case and he was awarded £20,000 in damages; he then sued for divorce in the Consistory Court of the Bishop of London and the final decree was granted on the 7th July. By this time, however, Paget had sailed for Holland on military duty and Char, in need of 'protection', once again returned to her husband, much to Arthur Wellesley's disgust. As a result of this reunion, which proved only temporary, Char gave birth to another daughter, Emily[20], on the 4th March 1810. Before this event, and as happened in the earlier case of Lord Cadogan and Mary Churchill, Wellesley had introduced a private Bill in the House of Lords to dissolve the marriage to enable him to marry again; this was enacted on the 22nd February 1810. Six weeks later Lady Caroline instituted divorce proceedings against Paget and obtained a decree absolute in October; the following month she wed the Duke of Argyll.

Lord Paget, in turn then married Lady Charlotte, described in 1811 as

Without much beauty, without much cleverness, without any one particularly attractive quality that can be defin'd, this same Ly. Paget is the most fascinating of human beings to man or woman . . . she governs him despotically, and the only very Mark'd Nature of her Character is being over strict in the performance of all Religious duties . . . to see her you would imagine she was innocence itself – how strange![21]

Paget, at about the same time, wrote to his brother, Arthur: 'My Lady and I have just calculated that she has cost me £20,000 for the 1st divorce, £10,000 for the 2nd, and £1,000 a year for Her Grace [the new Duchess of Argyll] – and I must admit I find her [the new Lady Paget] a good and cheap bargain notwithstanding.'[22]

The duel over, George had returned to the calmer atmosphere of the *Crocodile*, away from the family turmoil.

CHAPTER VIII

Death of a Brother

Sir Arthur Wellesley arrived in Lisbon on 22nd April 1809 together with his staff, including Henry who was again to act as one of his aides-de-camp. Wellesley spent only two days assessing the situation before leaving to join his Anglo-Portuguese army, 125 miles to the north, at Coimbra. The decision was to rescue 'the favourite town of Oporto' from Marshal Soult and this objective was achieved on the 12th May when the French force and its commander fled for the Spanish border, inflicting reprisals on the peasantry as they went. Portugal was once again clear of the French. On the 30th May, Wellesley wrote to the septuagenarian Spanish Captain-General Don Gregorio Garcia de la Cuesta:

I now send to Your Excellency's head quarters two officers in my confidence, Lieutenant-Colonel Bourke of the quarter master general's department, and the Honourable Lieutenant-Colonel Cadogan, one of my aides de camp, in order to explain to your Excellency my sentiments, and ascertain those of your Excellency respecting the cooperation of the two armies under our command respectively, in an attack upon Marshal Victor, with a view to the destruction of his corps, if possible, or if not possible its removal from its threatening position on the frontier of Portugal and of Andalusia.[1]

The following day Wellesley reported to Lord Castlereagh, the Secretary of War, 'I have sent Colonel Bourke and Colonel Cadogan to Cuesta to arrange a plan of co-operation in an attack upon Victor.' Henry remained at Cuesta's headquarters at the Fort of Miravete, Almarez, a hundred miles south-west of Madrid until Wellesley arrived with his army in early July. The battle of Talavera, at which Henry was present, was

The Battle of Talavera, 1809

fought on the 27th and 28th July and, said Wellesley, who had lost over 5000 men in the process of putting the enemy to flight and killing 7000 of their number, 'Never was there such a Murderous Battle!' Pursuit was impossible for only Cuesta's troops were fresh enough and, as Wellesley later revealed, 'the Spanish troops are not in a state of discipline to attempt a manoeuvre'. A week later Wellesley heard rumours of the armistice of Znaim ending the fighting between the French and Austrians, who had been defeated by Napoleon early in July and, suspecting now that some greater weight of the French army would be directed against his depleted force, he decided to retreat to Portugal. In recognition of the victory Wellesley was, nonetheless, elevated to the peerage on the 16th September as Viscount Wellington of Talavera.

Earlier in the year, on the 21st/22nd May, the Austrians had beaten the French at the battle of Aspern-Essling, just outside Vienna. The British government, wishing to do something to encourage them and at the same time to take some punitive action against the French-held Antwerp shipyards, appointed Lord Chatham, brother of the late William Pitt, and Rear-Admiral Sir Richard Strachan to lead a joint military and naval expedition, which had been in the course of preparation but without objective for some time, to Holland. The immediate aim would be the destruction of enemy ships in the river Scheldt leading to Antwerp, and the redeployment of enemy troops away from the Austrian and Spanish fronts. By the beginning of August a fleet of 520 transports escorted by 42 ships of the line, 25 frigates and 60 smaller vessels, had landed an army of 40,000 men on the island of Walcheren.

The army was divided into three main columns, the central one commanded by Paget who was much relieved to be away from England at this time, and the investment of Flushing was soon completed. Co-operation between the military and naval commanders soon broke down, however, and by the time the joint force was ready to thrust at Antwerp, the port had been

The siege of Flushing, during the Walcheren Expedition, 1809

heavily reinforced. Flushing fell on the 18th August after a delayed bombardment and while the troops had been waiting for the artillery to be brought up they had begun to show the first signs of a malarial disease. Walcheren with its dykes and drains was the ideal breeding ground for the mosquitoes which carried the infection and that summer it was particularly hot and wet, a situation exacerbated by the French opening the sluices and flooding the trenches in which the troops were dug-in. Soon the dead were so numerous that it was necessary to bury them at night, without lights, 'lest the survivors should see them and despair'. On the 27th August the Quartermaster-General presented a paper to the senior commanding army officers in which he estimated that there were now 26,000 of the enemy in place to defend Antwerp, with a further 9000 enemy troops within a short march. The British force had been reduced, through disease, to 24,000 men. The taking of Antwerp was now deemed an impossibility and the order was given to withdraw.

As the evacuation got under way, George was appointed on the 16th September to the 32-gun frigate *Pallas*[2], which was joined to the Walcheren fleet. Thousands of the sick, dying and dead were now carried back across the North Sea. Lady Wellington lamented, 'The sight of the Fleet is as dreadful as it was magnificent some weeks ago.'[3] Castlereagh now found himself cast in the rôle of scapegoat both for what was generally regarded as the Walcheren disaster and for the retreat from Talavera, and he discovered that George Canning, the Foreign Secretary, had persuaded Portland to remove him from the Cabinet. As a result of the ensuing dissent the Government fell. Castlereagh accused Canning of duplicity and the two ministers fought a duel on Putney Heath in which Canning sustained a minor wound. A new Tory administration came into office on the 6th December, headed by Portland's Chancellor of the Exchequer, Spencer Perceval. The new Secretary for War was Lord Liverpool, Marquess Wellesley became Foreign Secretary, while Wellington's elder brother, William

Wellesley-Pole was appointed Irish Chief Secretary. By now the last of the British troops were being withdrawn from Walcheren and the experience that George had gained at Quiberon Bay and at Ferrol stood him in good stead. Commodore Edward Owen informed Sir Richard Strachan in late December that:

> On the morning of the 23d, I received your letter, acquainting me that you intended to quit Flushing on that day. I immediately made preparation likewise to withdraw. The boats assembled, and embarked the rear-guard of the army, under the direction of the Hon. Captain Cadogan; whilst the few remaining guns of Veere and Armuyden points were rendered useless, and every other article of stores was taken off. In the Hon. Captain Cadogan, of the *Pallas*, I found a most zealous second and supporter.[4]

As the new year of 1810 opened, Napoleon remained master of Western Europe. By the Treaty of Vienna signed the previous October, the Austrians had been forced to agree to humiliating peace terms whereby Napoleon would marry their Emperor's daughter, the Archduchess Marie-Louise; the barren Josephine, his first wife, had already been divorced. The marriage took place on the 2nd April. One black cloud on Napoleon's horizon, however, was the behaviour of Czar Alexander who had previously refused him his sister's hand (the Archduchess was a second choice) and who was now showing signs of breaching the Continental System. Anticipating, perhaps, a new front in the East, Napoleon decided to leave the Peninsular campaign in the hands of Marshal Masséna who had command of 350,000 troops in Spain.

Masséna's second-in-command, Marshal Ney, opened a new offensive on the 22nd July by investing the Spanish fortress of Ciudad Rodrigo, guarding a key gateway into northwest Portugal, with 30,000 troops. Wellington, whose army, now increased to 33,000, contained many new recruits, did not think the moment right for a general action, and accordingly Cuidad Rodrigo fell seven days later. Masséna then lay

The Duke of Wellington

siege to Almeida, the opposing fortress over the border in Portugal and this too was taken, on the 28th August. Masséna, with an army of 65,000 men, then took the road west to Viseu before veering south to Busaco to meet Wellington whose army, reinforced by the Portuguese, had now increased to 51,000. The battle took place on the 27th September and resulted in a resounding victory for Wellington who lost 1250 men compared with 4600 French dead. Wellington now made a tactical withdrawal south towards Lisbon and on the 8th

October his army entered the Lines of Torres Vedras (the old towers); three lines of defensive fortifications based upon natural obstacles constructed earlier, on Wellington's orders, across the Lisbon peninsula.

Henry's regiment, the 71st (later part of the Highland Light Infantry), now arrived in Lisbon from Cove in Scotland. It was time for him to leave the comparative comfort of staff headquarters and return to regimental duty in the company of his younger brother Edward, who had been commissioned captain in the 71st six weeks earlier. The regiment had been raised in 1777 as Lord Macleod's Highlanders and comprised mainly Highlanders from the Mackenzie country and Lowlanders from Glasgow. Its uniform was a scarlet jacket with buff facings, a feather bonnet and the 'breacan-an-Flheilidh' or belted plaid of six ells of double-width Mackenzie tartan. In its short history the regiment had travelled far and fought well, against the Dutch at the battle of Blueberg and against the Spanish in the capture of Buenos Aires; it had also taken part in the Walcheren expedition.

The 71st had come ashore at Lisbon and been billeted at various locations in and around the city, which did not favourably impress one soldier who 'was sickened every hour of the day with the smell of garlic and oil ... The town is a dungheap from end to end.' The same unknown diarist[5] then records the regiment's first Portuguese encounter with the enemy:

The men paraded in the grand square on the seventh day and marched in sections to the music of the bugles to join the army. We halted on the first night at a palace belonging to the Queen of Portugal called Safrea where we were joined by the Honourable Henry Cadogan our Colonel. Next day the 14th October 1810, we joined the army at Sabral de Montre Agraco (Sobral), a small town surrounded by hills. We had not been three hours in the town and were busy cooking, when the alarm sounded. There were nine British and three Portuguese regiments in the town. We were all drawn up, and remained under arms expecting every moment to receive the enemy whose skirmishers covered Windmill Hill. In about an hour the light companies of all the regiments were ordered out, alongst with the 71st. Colonel Cadogan called to us, at the foot of the hill, 'My lads, this is the first affair I have ever been in with you. Show me what you can do. Now or never!' We gave a hurra and advanced up the hill, driving their advance skirmishers before us, until about halfway up, when we commenced a heavy fire and were as hotly received. In the meantime the remaining regiments evacuated the town. The enemy pressed so hard upon us, we were forced to make the rest of our way down the hill and were closely followed by the French through the town and up Gallows Hill. We got behind a mud wall and kept our ground in spite of their utmost effort. Next morning by day-break there was not a Frenchman to be seen. As soon as the sun was fairly up we advanced into the town and began a search for provisions which were now becoming very scarce.

The 'mud wall' was in fact a high wall which the oldest soldier of the regiment, John Rae, was unable to climb so he stood his ground, shot one Frenchman and bayoneted two others before, with assistance, he was able to clamber to safety. With the approval of the brigadier and Henry, both of whom had seen the incident, Rae was presented with an inscribed silver medal by his comrades.

Wellington now withdrew his forces from Sobral, moving them three miles south to a strongly fortified camp on the heights of Monte Agraco and here they remained until the 5th March, 1811, when it was discovered that Masséna, under cover of a dense fog, had struck camp and was moving north; the Lines of Torres Vedras had proved impregnable. Wellington set off in pursuit and the 71st was constantly in action against the French rearguard commanded by Marshal Ney. There was much privation and hardship before Masséna, on the 3rd May, launched a major attack upon the British centre at the village of Fuentes de Onoro, twenty miles south-east of Almeida. The defenders were driven up to the crags and Wellington, only now returned from a reconnaissance in the south and south-west, directed the 71st and the 79th, to recapture

The Battle of Fuentes de Onoro, 1811

the village. Henry on getting his orders called to his men, 'You have had nothing to eat for two days. There's biscuits and rum in that village. Come and get it!' The 71st, exhausted from having covered sixty miles without food in the previous three days, went into action. 'At 'em, 71st,' shouted Henry, 'Charge 'em down the Gallowgate! (a street in Glasgow).'⁶ The 71st led the way and after a bloody struggle, ejected the enemy who then counter-attacked with fresh troops. Henry's men were now reinforced by the 79th and the fighting continued until the narrow, labyrinthine streets of the village became so encumbered with the dead and wounded that the conflict came to a near standstill. A flag of truce was arranged and the French withdrew, taking their wounded with them. The 71st now enjoyed a far from sustaining meal, not of biscuit and rum, but four ounces of bread apiece 'collected out of the haversacks of the Foot Guards'. One hundred and twenty seven of their number had been killed in the fighting and now, with less than 200 effective troops, the regiment was temporarily out of action. Wellington sent his compliments for their conduct. Henry wrote to his brother-in-law Gerald Wellesley

Death of a Brother

Your letter of the 1st June gave me sincere pleasure. I assure you my dear Gerald that you don't mistake me when you suppose I must be gratified by the applause and approbation of those I love and I am indeed repaid for any exertion or zeal I may have shown in this interesting cause and against the infernal enemies that oppose it, by the public notice which has already been taken of my conduct. There is no reflection however that gives me such pleasure as that this conduct has been instrumental in bringing George his ship [the *Havannah*, see Chapter IX] and affecting by this means a permanent good to another.

I am most heartily rejoiced that you give such good account of yourself and your health my dear friend. May God preserve you for many years. You have objects to live for while I have none of the same tender interest and therefore my life is less worth preserving either for myself or others.

I have always thought and still more and more do I think that the man who at anytime of life is carried off in the field of battle has lived long enough and died most gloriously. I should not perhaps think so if I had any ties that made life more valuable to me than it is at present – at the same time as long as I am a soldier I trust these feelings will be never altered. Certainly the greatest gratification in life is the thought that one may be remembered and regretted in such a death and from the false reports that were lately in circulation about me I have had a delightful proof that this would be my case.

It is not the highest test of merit and the greatest of all comforts for those who loved James Pulteney, that his memory is so respected, his fate so universally lamented as his has been! Alas! I have been sensibly affected at this loss, which has at once deprived me of the person I loved almost better than any other, and of all the future prospects I had formed of amusement and happiness. Though my sorrow has been very silent, I do assure you my dear Gerald that no event in my life ever gave me more uneasiness and deep regret. This is a subject that has so fastened upon me, that I cannot help mixing it up into my thoughts as I have communicated them to paper in the other pages. So you must allow for the feelings I write under and don't for Heavens sake let them be shown to others who are less able than yourself to understand them.

I have received letters from Louisa and Charlotte, as well as many other people of late which have given me such gratification. Considering how little was said by Lord Wellington about my conduct, it is deeply gratifying to think that others have done me complete justice.

I have been writing to Cooke to get me an upper servant in Kaye's place. My present groom succeeded him but I want him for my stable entirely so you would greatly oblige me by assisting me to get a man of this description and to whom I would give any wages under two guineas a year if he suited me after a month's trial. C. Hammerly will finally approve and forward any servant out for me to the care of S. Hunter Esq., Paymaster at Lisbon. You will have heard the enemy have been dispersing these last five days towards Seville and Alcantara. The allied camp is expected to break up and go into Cantonments in this neighbourhood shortly. The future planning of the campaign must be uncertain, but all looks well for our cause. Lord Wellington's friendship to me is very great and tends to make this service doubly enjoyable. I wrote to Louisa a note lately and told her to send me some snuff handkerchiefs.

I will write to Charlotte very soon. All things will come right I think. The children will accept. Lord Wellington seems to expect Lord P. in this country. God bless you all.[7]

The 71st eventually received a draft of 350 recruits and when it became fully operational again it was joined to a force commanded by General Sir Rowland Hill, a veteran of Talavera and Busaco, whose orders were to hinder the activities of Marshal Soult in the Estremadura region south-west of Madrid. Hill waged a brilliant campaign and on the 19th May 1812 he destroyed the French pontoon bridge at Almarez on the Tagus, severing all communications between Soult and Marshal Marmont whose army was camped to the north, in the region of Almeida. The 71st again proved their worth in close action and more than once as they marched and counter-marched, they came within earshot of Wellington's guns laying siege to Badajoz, which the Spanish had surrendered to the French the previous year. On each occasion Henry, who had somehow obtained a supply of rum, ordered both officers and men to drink upstanding to 'the valour of the stormers and the success of British arms'. Badajoz was taken by Wellington on the 6th April so that, with the fortresses of Elvas, Almeida, and Cuidad Rodrigo already under British control, Portugal was now safe from invasion. Wellington could concentrate his efforts on expelling the French from Spain and he proceeded to inflict defeat upon Marmont's army at the battle of Salamanca on the 22nd July. In recognition of this victory he was created a Marquess and granted £100,000 by Parliament towards a future home; the Spanish Cortes created him Generalissimo of all their forces. Wellington, however, now encountered the combined forces of Soult and Joseph Bonaparte and in November he had no alternative other than to retreat to winter quarters at Ciudad Rodrigo, being joined on the way by the 71st and the rest of Hill's division. All Spain south of the river Tagus was now rid of French forces and those which remained in the north were harried by the local guerillas. Wellington's army, after a year of much successful

The storming of Badajoz, 1812

The Battle of Salamanca, 1812

action, needed to rest and recover its strength ready for the push into Napoleon's heartland.

During the winter months reinforcements arrived at Ciudad Rodrigo and by mid-May 1813 Wellington was ready to take the offensive with an army of 70,000 British, Spanish and Portuguese troops. Wellington and Hill marched north-west to Salamanca taking 30,000 men, including the 71st with Henry still in command, with the aim of convincing the French that this was the Allies' main thrust. The division arrived at its destination on the 28th May and on the next day Wellington quietly departed, leaving Hill in command, to meet up with General Sir Thomas Graham who was heading north with the remaining division of 40,000 men to outflank the French defences to the north-west of Salamanca. Wellington met Graham on the 30th May and they marched west to Toro, 40 miles north of Salamanca, to join up with Hill's division which had advanced there for the rendezvous. The French, now led by Joseph Bonaparte, were outflanked and Wellington had concentrated his force. Joseph duly ordered his army of 57,000 troops to retreat east along the Royal Road to France, thinking perhaps that the Allied army would simply pursue him. Wellington opted instead for another flanking movement and marched his army north-east, with the French border south-west of Bayonne as its target, safe in the know-

[127]

ledge that with the Navy's ascendancy at sea he could use the port of Santander on the Bay of Biscay as the entry point for essential supplies. Eventually realising Wellington's tactics, Joseph decided against the advice of his chief of staff, Marshal Jourdan, to make a stand behind the River Zadorra to the west of Vittoria, eighty miles from the French border.

On the morning of the 21st June the battle lines were drawn under a clouded sky; Joseph, in anticipation of a frontal assault, had drawn up his army in three defensive lines. Wellington was not to be so obliging, however, and he divided his force into four divisions; Hill would command on the right, Wellington the centre, Lord Dalhousie the left-centre and General Sir Thomas Graham on the left. The objective was to cut-off Joseph's retreat along the Royal Road in another flanking manoeuvre and to destroy his army. At about 8 o'clock the opening shots were fired when Hill sent a Spanish regiment, commanded by General Pablo Morillo, to sieze the steeply inclined Heights of Puebla from the French to

The Battle of Vittoria, 1813

enable Hill to attack the enemy on their left flank on the plain below. The heights were quickly secured but immediately re-captured by a French counter-attack. The 71st was then sent in and during the desperate hand-to-hand fighting that ensured, Henry fell from his horse, mortally wounded.[8]

Three days later Wellington reported the sad news to his brother Gerald:

You will see by my despatch sent to England this day that poor Henry Cadogan fell in the Battle of the 21st inst near Vittoria and although the object of this letter is to urge you to break this misfortune to his sisters and friends I can find nothing to console you for the loss we have all sustained excepting the occasion on which he fell, and his peculiar zeal then and upon all other occasions which offered themselves.

I cannot express to you how much I feel for this loss, let alone on private grounds. He was an officer of the greatest zeal and promise and attached to his profession enthusiastically. After he was mortally wounded and knew that he was dying, he desired that he might be carried to a spot from which he could see the operations of the day and he did live to witness the total defeat of the enemy.

I can write no more on this distressing subject. Pray give my best love to Emily and believe me, Ever Yours affectionately, Wellington.[9]

On the 30th June one of Henry's brother officers in the 71st, Lieutenant Alexander Duff, wrote a detailed description of Henry's death to his brother George:

As it may be some consolation to you to be informed of the circumstances attending the last moments of your truly noble brother, our late gallant and much lamented Commander, I am induced to commit them to paper in the order in which they occurred in hopes that a knowledge of the admirable manner in which he died may in some measure tend to alleviate your grief for his loss.

About ten o'clock on the morning of the 21st our Battalion was ordered to support a Spanish Regiment which was engaged with the enemy's skirmishers on the top of a high hill immediately on our right. The head of our column had scarcely gained the top of the heights when we found ourselves in close contact with a battalion of the Enemy who were advancing au pas du charge. Your gallant brother immediately ordered us to charge and led us on in his usual manner. The enemy gave way, and we followed, animated by the gallant example of our leader, when a fatal shot deprived us of him, you of a brother, and the army of a hero.

He constantly felt that his wound would prove mortal, and would not permit those who had gathered round him, to remove him from the field, but desired them to carry him to the top of a neighbouring precipice, from whence he could have a birds-eye view of the whole of the approaching battle. He repeatedly said, as he was borne along, that he could not die happier, that it was the death he always wished to meet, and that he would die perfectly satisfied.

About an hour afterwards I returned to the spot where he was lying and sat down close beside him. Paymaster McKenzie, Surgeon Logan and Mr Gavin were standing round him, their countenances were expressive of fearful anxiety. There were also some French wounded and some prisoners near where he lay, amongst the latter Colonel Berlier, who commanded the Regiment opposed to us.

Soon after I arrived at the spot the Colonel raised his head and asked me if I was wounded? I answered that I was. He then asked if there were any other casualties amongst the officers? and I replied that Mr. Richards was the only other, I knew of, that was wounded, to which he replied 'thank God!' and again laid down his head on the knees of his servant. Lieutenant-Colonel Cother now arrived, also wounded. Colonel Cadogan had seen and admired the very gallant conduct of Lieutenant-Colonel Cother. On learning therefore from the Paymaster that he had come back wounded, he, after a long pause, and very faintly, said 'bless him! bless him!'. These were the last words he spoke, and it was too evident that life was fast ebbing. He however once more raised his head and looked with a very languid eye towards the battle which had now become pretty general along the line. I observed to him that the enemy was beaten at all points, and I thought I perceived a faint smile on his countenance, but this might have been imagination, as I knew it would be the most welcome intelligence that could reach his dying ear. He again laid down his head, closed his eyes and appeared to be falling asleep. I watched his countenance narrowly, he breathed freely, and seemed

'The heroic death of Col Cadogan'

to enjoy a tranquil slumber: and notwithstanding, Mr. Gavin, myself and his servant were looking earnestly on his face, we could not
perceive the exact moment at which he ceased to breath, no struggle, no groan, not even the slightest sign announced his dissolution,
'he died as die the brave' and we may justly say of him as a soldier
what Tickell said of Addison as a Christian.

Death of a Brother

He taught us how to live, and ah! too high
A price for learning, taught us how to die!

He expired about ten minutes before four o'clock, on the evening of the 21st June, a day glorious to our army, but to none more than him we lament.

We removed his body that night to a village called Sovejana de Alava, where I remained with it until the next evening, when Captain W.A. Grant arrived with a party of men to assist at his funeral.

After the body was cleaned of the coagulated blood and clean linen put on, it was sewed up in a blanket, it was carried to the grave, on a bier which we obtained from the village church, by six of the soldiers, Captain Grant, Myself and his private servant attending. His remains lie interred in a deep grave, on the field of battle, in a spot that had never been tilled, about a quarter of a mile to the north east of the village of Sovejana, and six miles to the southward and eastward of Vittoria.

We collected ammunition on the spot and fired three rounds over his grave, and I hope you will believe that every honour was paid to his remains, which the circumstances we were placed in admitted of. I cannot conclude this letter without recommending to your notice John Robertson, private servant to your late lamented brother, whose affectionate attention to his master after he was wounded, the deep and sincere sorrow he shewed at his death, and the pious care he took of his remains, excited my warm admiration.

He is charged with the Colonel's last adieus to you and your sisters and will deliver you a portion of the Colonel's hair which I directed him to cut off after his death.[10]

It was later recorded that Henry died 'without ever having been married'.[11] On the 4th August 1832, Wellington was to write to Lieutenant-General Sir Edward Barnes, Commander-in-Chief of the forces in the East Indies, recommending to him 'Henry Carr, an officer in the service of the East India Company on the Bengal establishment. Carr is the son of the late Colonel Cadogan of the Seventy-First Regiment of Foot'.[12]

CHAPTER IX

Zara and Goodbye

On Wednesday the 4th April 1810, George donned his full-dress uniform, now bearing a second epaulette to mark his three years' seniority in post rank, picked up his gold-laced hat and his sword and went out to a waiting postchaise for the short drive to Hampton Court Palace in the company of his friend and supporter, John Danbury. There they were met by the palace Chaplain, Gerald Wellesley who, before a small gathering of family, friends and brother-officers, officiated at George's marriage to Miss Honoria Louisa Blake, the youngest daughter of the late Joseph and Honoria Blake of Ardfry, County Galway, and a descendant of Richard Blake, a soldier of fortune who had accompanied Prince John to Ireland in 1185 in much the same circumstances which had prompted George's great-great-grandfather Major William Cadogan to cross the Irish Sea with the Earl of Strafford in 1633. Honoria's eldest brother Joseph had been created an Irish peer in 1800 as Baron Wallscourt of Ardfry and following his death three years later the title had passed to Honoria's nephew, another Joseph Blake. The marriage settlement which took effect upon the completion of the ceremony had been entered into two days earlier and this recorded that by virtue of the marriage settlement agreed by his parents, George was entitled, as one of the six surviving children, to the sum of £2500 while Honoria under her father's will had a legacy of £4000. It was agreed that George should have £2000 from his intended wife's inheritance to dispose of as he saw fit, with the remainder of their joint capital worth being used to set up a trust for the eventual benefit of any children of the marriage. In the meantime, the income would accrue firstly to George then, upon his death, to Honoria. The formalities and celebrations concluded, George was then able, with the express permission of his commanding admiral, to enjoy a few days' shore-leave before returning to duty. Honoria took up residence at Downham Hall in the company of Lady Louisa and there on the following 9th January she gave birth to a daughter, Augusta Sarah.

George remained with the Channel fleet when, on the 6th June 1811, he took command of one of the more heavily armed fifth-rates, the 42-gun newly built frigate *Havannah*, taking with him his first lieutenant William Hamley who had also served George in a similar capacity on board the *Crocodile*. Hamley obtained a commendation from his captain in a letter dated 7th September 1811, addressed to the fleet commander and subsequently published in the London Gazette:

SIR,

Some of the enemy's coasting vessels having taken shelter under a battery of three twelve-pounders on the south-west side of the Penmarks, I yesterday morning sent my first lieutenant (William Hamley), with the boats of this ship, to spike the guns, and bring them out or destroy them; which service he performed, according to the subjoined list, without the loss of a man, in a manner that does great credit to himself, as well as all the officers and men employed upon the occasion.

L'Aimable Fanny, schooner, laden with wine and brandy, taken.
St. Jean, chasse marée, laden with salt, taken.
Le Petit Jean Baptiste, chasse marée, laden with wine and brandy, taken,
Le Buonaparte, chasse marée, laden with wine and brandy, taken.
Le Voltigeur, chasse marée, laden with wine and brandy, taken.
Chasse marée, name unknown, laden with wine and brandy, dismantled and set fire to, afterwards extinguished.[1]

During the ensuing autumn, as George continued to operate off the French coast, Mary Churchill died at Nancy in her sixty-second year. Administration of her will was granted in

January 1812 to Sir William Cooper's brother Frederick, with a note that the former cleric was then 'detained as a prisoner in France'.[2] Mary's father, Colonel Churchill, turned ninety, outlived his youngest daughter, and died at his house in Grosvenor Street on the 13th April 1812. In his will, drawn-up in 1807, there is no mention of Mary and all the property and monies arising from the by now late Lady Mary Churchill's marriage settlement, 'over which I have a power of appointment or disposition'[3], passed to Mary's brother Horace. Perhaps, after all, Sir William Cooper did not receive his financial reward. Certainly there would be some delay before Mary's daughters wore their mother's diamonds.

Lord Uxbridge died on the 13th March and the family earldom now passed to Lord Paget. The earlier understandable hostility of the Paget family to the former Lady Charlotte was generally subsiding for, as Lord Galloway wrote to his brother-in-law Arthur Paget nine months earlier:

If your daughter should elope with a man offensive to you, I do not suppose you would speedily be reconciled, and yet I do not suppose you would determine never to be reconciled. Feelings extremely shocked require *Time* to recover, as well as Time to manifest the probable permanent conduct of the other party.... I can easily conceive Lady Ux. refusing intercourse now, and yet after P[aget] and his Wife have lived long enough together and as amicably and respectably as possible, being disposed to bury in oblivion Present events.... This is so much the constant practice of the world in *all Extreme Cases* that we must conclude it to be natural, and consequently correct.[4]

The new Lady Uxbridge, having given birth to another son, Clarence, in 1811, was now expectant again. The career of her former husband, now Sir Henry Wellesley K.B., had progressed and he had been appointed Ambassador to the Court of Spain where he was using all his diplomatic skills to persuade the Cortes to create his brother Wellington, Generalissimo of all their forces. Sir Henry had refused to admit paternity of Lady Charlotte's son Gerald and he was now in the care of Lady Wellington. Lady Emily's union had been blessed with a further three daughters, Georgiana, Mary and – in the days when it was more a girl's name – Cecil. George and Honoria had also added to their family with the birth on the 15th February of a son and heir, Henry, at the Churchill house in South Audley Street.

Napoleon's foreboding had proved correct and Tsar Alexander breached the Continental System and authorised renewed trade with Britain. Napoleon as a result was in the throes of making military preparations for the invasion of Russia, and as part of a new strategy, he had during the spring of 1812 forged alliances with both Prussia and Austria. At home on the 11th May in the lobby of the House of Commons Spencer Perceval was shot dead by a merchant whose business had been ruined by the war and Lord Liverpool became the new Prime Minister with Lord Castlereagh, who had returned to the government only three months earlier, as Foreign Secretary. The new administration's burden was immediately increased when on the 18th June the United States of America, incensed by British handling of neutral shipping, declared war on Britain. Six days later Napoleon crossed the River Niemen from Poland and invaded Russia with an army of 700,000 men. He returned in less than six months, beaten by a combination of Russian resolve and Russian winter; only 20,000 of his Grande Armée got back to France and in the meantime Britain had made peace with Tsar Alexander.

During the course of 1812 George was sent, still in command of the *Havannah*, to join the Mediterranean Fleet commanded since the spring of 1811 by Pellew, now Vice-Admiral, whose flag flew in the 120-gun *Caledonia*. Sir Edward, after service on board the *Tonnant*, had been promoted Rear-Admiral in April 1804 and appointed Commander-in-Chief in the East Indies, where he remained until 1809, returning home to be Commander-in-Chief of the North Sea Fleet, where he remained until sailing south. The *Havannah* was subsequently attached to the Adriatic Squadron commanded by Rear-

HMS Curacoa *(centre) and* Havannah *(left) standing in to reconnoitre the French Fleet in Toulon harbour. Winter of 1812*

Admiral Thomas Fremantle who, as captain of the *Nèptune*, had fought at Trafalgar. The squadron comprised three ships of the line and seven frigates and its rôle was to harass the French occupying the 'Illyrian Provinces', so named by Napoleon in 1809 and comprising the former, mainly Venetian, provinces of Dalmatia, Croatia, Görz, Ragusa, Carniola, Istria and Carinthia. The Venetian territory had been ceded to Austria in 1797 and it remained part of The Empire until 1805 when, after the battle of Austerlitz, it was absorbed initially into Napoleon's kingdom of Italy, depriving Austria entirely of her seaboard and improving French communications with the Near East. Vis, the outermost of the Dalmatian islands, was occupied in 1811 by an English naval force under Captain William Hoste and shortly after this the islands of Korcula, Hvar and Lagosta were also taken. The islands together were now a valuable centre for smuggling English goods into Dalmatia and beyond, despite a French blockade.

[137]

George had to wait until the opening of the New Year for his first notable action in the squadron, which he reported to Captain Charles Rowley of the *Eagle* for transmission firstly to Fremantle and thence, in accordance with usual practice, to John Wilson Croker, the Secretary to the Admiralty:

In reporting the capture of the enemy's gun-boat, No. 8, of one long 24-pounder, and 35 men, commanded by Monsieur Joseph Floreus, enseigne de vaisseau, I must beg leave to call your attention to the great skill and gallantry with which this service was executed by the first lieutenant, William Hamley, the officers and men under his orders, who, with only a division of this ship's boats, at two o'clock in the afternoon of the 6th instant, attacked and carried the above vessel, far superior to them in force, prepared in every respect, and supported by musketry from the shore, where she was made fast: our boats not having an expectation of meeting an armed vessel, till (upon opening the creek where she lay) they were fired upon, and desired by the troops on shore to surrender. I have to lament the loss of a very fine young man, Mr Edward Percival, master's mate, killed, and two seamen, wounded. Three merchant vessels were also taken.[5]

Four weeks later there was further action:

Vice-admiral Sir Edw. Pellew has also transmitted a letter from the Hon. Captain Cadogan, of his Majesty's ship the *Havannah*, to Rear-adm. Fremantle, giving an account of the destruction, on the 7th of February, of an Enemy's convoy of 25 sail, 4 of them gun-boats, by the boats of the *Havannah*, under Lieutenant Hamley, on the coast of Manfredonia. A battery of 7 guns was destroyed by the marines, and two of the vessels brought out, the rest scuttled and left full of water. The convoy came from Venice, and the vessels were laden with ordnance stores. This service was performed without the loss of a man.[6]

George then had occasion, on March 27th and June 29th, to report two further actions direct to Fremantle:

I have the honour to inform you, that, in executing our orders of the 10th instant, the boats of this ship have been twice successfully employed against the enemy's trade; once on the morning of the

22nd instant, in the capture of a large trabacolo of three nine-pounders and small arms, and the destruction by fire of a similar vessel, laden with oil, under the town of Vasto; and again yesterday morning, in the capture of five armed trabacolos, and five feluccas laden with salt, near the town of Fortore. In both instances, the vessels being hauled aground, completely dismantled, and under the protection of a strong body of military on the beach, besides the guns of the latter vessels, which had been landed. I ordered my boats to land wide of the sport, and force their position; this was immediately effected (under a strong opposition) by Lieutenant Hamley, first of this ship (the marines, under Lieutenant Hockly, very judiciously posted), whilst the vessels were equipped and got afloat by the exertions of the officers and men, with a celerity that reflects the highest credit on their characters. At Vasto, the French officer who headed the troops was killed. At Fortoro, the enemy left one man killed. I am happy to say, we have only two men very slightly wounded.[7]

I have the honour to report the capture of an armed convoy of the enemy's, consisting of ten sail, under the town of Vasto, on the morning of the 27th inst. by the boats of this ship, commanded by my first lieutenant, William Hamley.

The enemy being apprized of our approach the preceding day, had assembled in force, and taken every possible precaution to prevent our getting their vessels off; but having landed to the right, and forced them from their guns (eight in number), we remained masters of the spot the whole day, until the vessels were rigged and got afloat. This little service has been performed with the spirit ever manifest in Lieutenant Hamley, my officers, and ship's company generally, and with only three men slightly wounded, while the enemy acknowledged six killed and seven wounded.[8]

George now received news of Henry's death. Wellington had carried the day at Vittoria although Joseph had escaped over the Pyrenees back into France with 55,000 of his men, while the Allied troops were preoccupied plundering the French baggage train. The battle was nonetheless a great personal triumph for Wellington who was immediately raised to the rank of Field Marshal by the Prince Regent (the Prince of

Wales had come to the regency in February 1811 when his father, King George had lapsed into irreparable insanity). In his despatch from Vittoria, Wellington wrote:

I am concerned to have to report, that Lieut.-Col. Cadogan has died of a wound which he received. In him his Majesty has lost an officer of great zeal and tried gallantry, who had already acquired the respect and regard of the whole profession, and of whom it might be expected, that if he had lived he would have rendered the most important services to his country.[9]

Viscount Castlereagh said in the House of Commons on the 13th July:

that it had been generally the rule to confine motions for the erection of Monuments to the memory of those who had died in the service of their Country to cases in which the thanks of Parliament had been voted; but there were in the present case peculiar considerations for paying the debt of national gratitude to some distinguished officers, who, though not holding the rank of General Officers, had yet exercised high military commands.

There was no mode in which we could more beneficially lay out the true treasures of the Nation, than in placing monuments in our national edifices to the honour and memory of our brave officers. On the wise adoption of this practice much depended, both for strength, security, and character of this Country, and perhaps for the security of the world. His Lordship then moved four addresses to the Prince Regent, for the erection of monuments to the memory of Major Gen. Bowles, who fell in the assault at Salamanca, on the 17th June, 1812; to Major-Gen. Brock, who fell on the 16th October, 1812, at Kingstown, in Upper Canada; to Sir W. Myers, who commanded a brigade at the battle of Albuera, and fell on the 16th May, 1812, and to Col. the Hon. Henry Cadogan, who lost his life at the memorable victory of Vittoria.[10]

Seven days later George had again to sit down in his cabin with pen and paper:

Subjoined is the statement of the result of an attack made by this ship, [*Havannah*] and H.M. Sloop *Partridge,* upon a small convoy,

[140]

Monument to Henry Cadogan in St Paul's Cathedral

seven in number, on the N.W. coast of Manfredonia, on the morning of the 18th inst.

1 Neapolitan gun-boat, 1 eighteen pounder, captured.
1 Neapolitan gun-boat, 1 eighteen pounder, burnt.
1 pinnace, with 1 six pounder, destroyed.
2 armed trabacolos, of 3 guns each, laden with salt, captured,
2 armed trabacolos, of 3 guns each, laden with salt, destroyed.
The gun-boats quite new, and belonging to the fifth division.[11]

The war permitted scant time for mourning.

The news for Napoleon worsened as the year wore on. In February, Prussia defected and made an alliance with Russia and they extended an invitation to Austria and Britain to join them in a Fourth Coalition. On the 17th March Prussia declared war on France; in June came the battle of Vittoria and in August an Austrian declaration of war was followed by a French defeat at the hands of the Russians at Kulm. In early

[141]

October Wellington's army crossed into southern France and later in the month Napoleon was soundly beaten by four Allied armies at the battle of Leipzig, forcing his retreat to France. Castlereagh was sent to Germany in December with full powers to give assistance to the Allies and a general invasion of France began. The writing was on the wall for the Emperor Napoleon.

The Adriatic squadron continued to contribute its part to what had now developed into a final thrust against the enemy and in October the port of Trieste was taken. In the ensuing months George was sent to assist the Austrian army in the reduction of Zara, a redoubtable and ancient fortress on the Dalmatian coast mounting 110 guns, 7 large mortars and 11 howitzers, and garrisoned by 2000 veteran troops under the command of Baron Roisé. Two letters remain to bring an end to George's active naval career: the first is from him to Rear-Admiral Fremantle, dated December 6th, 1813

It is with great satisfaction I have the honour to inform you, that the fortress of Zara has this day capitulated to the combined Austrian and English forces, after sustaining a cannonade of thirteen days from the English batteries, consisting of two 32-pound carronades, eight 18-pounders, and seven 12-pound long guns, as well as two howitzers worked by Austrians.

As the courier which conveys this information will set out immediately, I shall defer entering into particulars until another opportunity, and confine myself to the general terms granted, which are, that the garrison are to march out with honours of war; to ground their arms on the glacis, and then to be conducted as prisoners of war, until exchanged, to the outposts of the nearest French army.

The outwork of the garrison to be occupied this evening by the Austrian troops, and the whole of the enemy to march out on the 9th, at ten A.M.

As soon as I can make ready a copy of the terms, I shall have the honour of forwarding them to you:

The second is a Letter from Rear-Admiral Fremantle, to John Wilson Croker.

Zara and Goodbye

I have the honour of enclosing a report from the Hon. Captain Cadogan, of H.M.S. *Havannah*, giving an account of the surrender of the very important fortress of Zara to the Austrian and British forces.

The judgment, perseverance, and ability shewn by him, on every occasion, will not, I am persuaded, escape their Lordships' observation.

Captain Cadogan, with the crews of a frigate and a sloop, has accomplished as much as required the services of the squadron united at Trieste.[12]

George came ashore for the last time on the 31st December 1813, a little over eighteen years since he had first gone on board the *Indefatigable*; he had spent sixteen of his thirty years at war. It was time for a quieter life.

CHAPTER X

Baron Oakley of Caversham

It must have been evident to George for the past twelve months or more that a lasting peace was not far off and he was viewing with mixed feelings the prospects of life in a peace-time Navy, even assuming that he would be able to retain his present command or find a new one, when once again ships by the hundred would be laid-up and their captains beached. There were times, no doubt, when on his ordered quarter-deck, he wanted to continue the seagoing life he had known since boyhood, while on other occasions, when the captain's burden was weighing especially heavy, he longed to escape to Downham to enjoy the company of his growing family; Honoria had recently presented him with another daughter, Honoria Louisa. Henry's death had decided him, for with Lord Cadogan's continuing infirmity he was now effectively heir to the earldom and the estates. He had a new responsibility: the survival of the family inheritance. There was of course Edward, but he was as yet unmarried and still serving actively with the 71st. It was a *choix forcé*; he would leave the Navy at the earliest opportunity.

A Fourth Coalition came about on the 1st March 1814 when Britain, Austria, Prussia and Russia signed the Treaty of Chaumont. Each of the Allies agreed not to make a separate peace with Napoleon and to continue the war until France was returned to her boundaries of 1791. Britain also agreed to provide a subsidy of £5 million to the Allies. Before the month was out Wellington had occupied Bordeaux while Tsar Alexander and King Frederick William of Prussia had entered Paris. Napoleon abdicated and, by the Treaty of Fontainebleau signed on the 11th April, he renounced all claims to the French, Italian and Austrian crowns in exchange for a pension of two million francs and the Principality of Elba, where he landed on the 3rd May. Wellington on the same day was raised to a dukedom and within twenty-four hours he rode on a white horse into Paris in time for a grand parade of Allied troops before the restored Bourbon monarch, Louis XVIII. In December the war with America also came to an end.

The contribution made by George at the capture of Zara was recognised on the 22nd July when he was made a Knight of the Imperial Military Order of Maria Theresa, 'in testimony of the high sense which the Emperor of Austria entertains of the distinguished gallantry displayed by him (in co-operation with the Imperial Troops), on the coast of The Adriatic'. The award of the Knight's Cross was made earlier by the Emperor in a decree to his Foreign Minister:

DEAR PRINCE METTERNICH
I wish Major-General Tomassich to be awarded the Commander's Cross of The Military Order of Maria Theresa and for Colonel Widmayer of the Liccaner Regiment and Second Lieutenant Krap-freiter of the Artillery together with the British Royal Navy Captain George Cadogan, who are all with General Tomassich in Dalmatia, to be awarded the Knight's Cross of this Order for outstanding distinction in the face of the enemy; you are now to instigate the necessary further action.
Frieburg 26th December 1813 FRANZ[1]

The presentation took place in Vienna early in the new year and the arrangements were made known to George in a letter from the Duke of Wurtemberg:

Vienna, 8th January 1814
SIR,
I am pleased to inform you that His Majesty the Emperor of Austria has charged me to bestow upon you the Knights Cross of The Military Order of Maria Theresa. His Majesty awards this decoration in recognition of your glorious achievements and in

particular of the important services which you contributed at the capture of Zara.

As required by the Statutes of the Order the troops under my command will be present at the ceremony when I will have the honour to present you with the Cross, so that they may be reminded of your merits and inspired to glory with our brothers-in-arms from your Nation. I invite you to be at the Prater, on horseback, tomorrow morning at ten o'clock and to take your position with the right wing of the cavalry which will be in battle formation.

I have the honour to be your very humble and very devoted servant.

FERDINAND,
Duke of Wurtemberg, Marshal.[2]

Pellew was not forgotten in the matter of honours and some few weeks before George received his Knight's Cross he was raised to the peerage as Baron Exmouth of Canonteign, a Devon estate bought with his hard-earned prize money.

Napoleon was not to remain long in exile; ten months after stepping ashore he escaped from Elba and returned to Paris, putting Louis to flight. By the 16th of June 1815 he had reassumed command of the French army and defeated the Prussians at Ligny. Two days later, however, he was defeated by an Allied army commanded by Wellington at Waterloo.

The anticipated lasting peace had arrived and George and Honoria were in residence at Downham Hall with their four children; the youngest, George, was seven months old. Lady Louisa, now 27, and seemingly a determined spinster, lived with them. George's income was about £1500 a year which, with the abolition of income tax in 1816, enabled him to live the comfortable life of a country gentleman; he went rarely to London and he did not attend a grand dinner given by the Prince Regent at Carlton House at which his brother-in-law the former Lord Uxbridge, now the Marquess of Anglesey, and Sir Henry Wellesley were guests. A relative of Wellesley wrote afterwards to record that the Prince took him and Castlereagh aside before dinner:

and said he was much distressed at Lord Anglesey and Henry being in the room together; that he had never recollected it till he saw them, etc., etc., and he desired me to take an opportunity of explaining to Henry that the circumstances had arisen from mere misadventure. I told him that I was sure Henry was quite easy about the matter, and I informed his R.H. that in a conversation I had lately had with Henry, he had observed that he now considered Lord Anglesey as the best friend he had ever had in his life. Castlereagh observed coolly that the meeting was a fortunate circumstance, for it would be impossible they should not very often meet, and therefore the sooner the thing was over the better; upon which P.R. observed that Castlereagh was the most impudent fellow existing, and so broke up the conversation. Henry did not seem at all annoyed at the meeting.[3]

Anglesey had received the marquessate in recognition of his successful command of the British cavalry at Waterloo, when he came under the orders of the man with whose sister-in-law he had eloped. There was evidently no residual rancour on the part of the Commander-in-Chief. At one stage in the battle Anglesey, concerned for Wellington's safety, galloped up and shouted, 'For God's sake, Duke, don't expose yourself so.' A moment later a cannon ball passed over the neck of Wellington's horse and shattered Anglesey's leg, which was subsequently amputated. Sir Henry had fared rather better and early in 1816 he married the eldest daughter of the Marquess of Salisbury.

George's financial position did not improve measurably until towards the end of 1821 when, with the death of his Great-Aunt Sarah, he became tenant-for-life of a moiety or one-half of the Chelsea Manor Estate, worth £3500 a year. The other half was vested in Lord Cadogan or, to be more precise, his 'committee', now comprised only of Lord Orford (formerly Horatio Lord Walpole) and Hans Sloane who at this time took the additional surname of Stanley in honour of his second-cousin Hans Stanley who had bequeathed to him an estate in Hampshire.

The Manor of Chelsea, which was first recorded during the reign of Edward the Confessor (1042–66), originally covered a triangular shaped piece of land bounded by the River Thames in the South, the River Bourne in the east, and the road leading from Fulham to Knightsbridge. George's Great-Grandfather, Sir Hans Sloane, bought what was generally regarded as the 'Manor of Chelsea' in 1712 from Lord Cheyne, supplementing this acquisition in 1737 by the purchase of Beaufort House from the Duke of Beaufort; his eventual estate, however, only covered about three-quarters of the original manor, the remaining acreage, including the ground for the Royal Hospital completed in 1691, having been sold separately, or comprising common land.

When Sir Hans died in 1753, he bequeathed one undivided moiety of the manor to his younger daughter Elizabeth, wife of the 2nd Baron Cadogan, and the other to his elder daughter Sarah, married to George Stanley, a landed gentleman of Hampshire. The Cadogan moiety had duly passed from Lady Cadogan to her husband, then to their son the 3rd Baron Cadogan who had ensured its passage to his son, the present Earl. The Stanley moiety was left by Sarah to her son Hans, a politician, diplomat and a former lord of the admiralty who in January 1780, during a visit to Earl Spencer at Althorp, had 'cut his throat with a penknife in the woods, and died before assistance could be obtained'.[4] In his will[5] Hans stipulated that the moiety should pass to his sisters, Anne, wife of Lord Mendip (the former Welbore Ellis) and Sarah married to another Member of Parliament, Christopher D'Oyley, and thence to their children with a proviso that should, on the death of the surviving sister, there be no surviving issue, the Stanley moiety would pass to the 3rd Baron Cadogan. The newly created 1st Earl Cadogan in his turn left all his landed property, with the exception of the Cadogan moiety, upon trust, for the use and benefit of his children by Mary Churchill and accordingly in February 1814 deeds of 'lease and release' were entered into, ensuring that in the circumstances provided

Hans Stanley   *Gerald Wellesley*

for by Hans Stanley the second moiety would pass to George. Both Stanley sisters died childless and so George came into the inheritance. Great-Aunt Sarah had also left him £1500 and Honoria £500; and she had written-off 'the principal and any interest that may be due on his bond'[6], a reference to an earlier loan.

In the intervening years, while George was awaiting the first part of his inheritance, various family occasions of greater or lesser happiness had come and gone. The year after Waterloo, Honoria's nephew Lord Wallscourt had died and was succeeded by another of her Blake nephews who, disturbingly for his guests, was prone to 'get half-crazed at times and very violent. He liked walking about the house with no clothes on, and ... carried a cow bell in his hand when in this state of nudity, so that the maid servants had warning of his approach.' He was eventually to die from cholera rather than the cold. Edward, in continuance of his military career, had purchased his majority in the 8th West Indian Regiment. Lord and Lady Anglesey's family continued to grow and by 1817,

[149]

when Lord Anglesey's eldest daughter, Lady Caroline, married the 1st Earl Cadogan's great-grandson, the 5th Duke of Richmond, they had another three children. Lady Emily had completed her family with a further two sons, but sixteen years of marriage to the 'impartial and conciliatory' Gerald Wellesley had proved too much for the Churchill in her personality and in 1818 the couple separated, which was to prove the death knell for this particular Wellesley's professional advancement. Honoria then appears to have had a dalliance with Henry de Ros, son of Lord Henry Fitzgerald, while in the year following another son, Horace, was born and died, shortly after the Prince Regent had acceded to the throne as George IV.

Lord Liverpool remained in office as Prime Minister although in 1822 he had need of a new Foreign Secretary when the Marquess of Londonderry (formerly Viscount Castlereagh) committed suicide. Like Hans Stanley he cut his throat, and was succeeded by his old duelling adversary George Canning. The appointment was resented by several members of Liverpool's Cabinet and they resigned; in the consequent reshuffle Sir Robert Peel, formerly the chief Secretary of Ireland, was given the office of Home Secretary. The British economy had recovered from the effects of the Napoleonic wars; internal trade was in a healthier state and export of home products into Europe, America and other countries, was thriving. These more prosperous days were naturally reflected in land and property values and in 1822 George and Lord Cadogan's trustees put in train two Private Acts of Parliament, both of which finally received Royal Assent on the 10th June 1825[7], to facilitate the further development of the Chelsea Manor estate, a process begun by Sir Hans Sloane, and continued by Lord Cadogan's father.

George and Honoria had one final addition to their family in 1821 with the birth of Frederick William, while within the next two years both Henry and George had departed Downham Hall for Eton College leaving Augusta and Honoria in the care of a governess. Their Uncle Edward at thirty-three and now on the half-pay list of the 8th West Indian Regiment, married Miss Ellen Donovan while Uncle Gerald Wellesley, continuing his ministry at Chelsea, was finding it impossible to advance in the church hierarchy. The Duke of Wellington had failed to convince Lord Liverpool as to the merits of his brother's case for the Irish bishopric of Cloyne, the Prime Minister taking the view that his separation from Lady Emily, notwithstanding her adultery and his refusal to divorce her, disqualified him from a bishopric. The Duke, who must by now if not before have grown thoroughly weary of the two Cadogan sisters, thought this 'hard punishment for having an adulterous wife', but Liverpool remained unmoved and Gerald, in 1824, became Rector of Bishop Wearmouh, County Durham and Canon of Durham Cathedral. Honoria, meanwhile, was enjoying the Paris season as related by Harriet Countess Granville to her sister Lady Carlisle:

My dearest Sis – We have this moment heard of the death of the Duke of York. I felt a great regard and liking for him when I saw him every day at breakfast at the Pavilion, and more so now when everybody agrees in the perfection of his conduct in the last trial of all. All the accounts received of his illness and the admirable patience and consideration for those about him add to the pity I feel for General Upton, C. Greville, and others of his friends, to whom his loss must be quite irreparable.

We shall now have a week or ten days of perfect rest and quiet, as we do not mean to go out any more till after the funeral, and then I hope black gloves will be an excuse for balls, etc.

I have been twice at the Duchesse de Berri's this week, at a concert and a children's ball, where Granville and Freddy were the happiest of the happy. They are going to-night to draw King and Queen at Mrs. Cadogan's.[8]

Lord Liverpool having been the prime cause of Gerald Wellesley's travelling north with his family, then died that same year and Canning became Prime minister. Wellington and Peel both refused to serve under him, fearing that he would try to carry a bill giving religious freedom to Catholics.

Canning too, however, died some few months later and he was succeeded by another Tory, Viscount Goderich, who achieved the dubious distinction of being Britain's only Prime Minister who never appeared before Parliament. In January 1828 Goderich left office and Wellington, in an attempt to hold together the disintegrating Tory ministry, moved into No. 10 Downing Street to discover that his actions served only to exacerbate the situation. During the following year Wellington, yielding to public pressure, carried the act of Parliament that achieved Catholic emancipation, without renouncing his personal belief that it would ultimately produce the destruction of English rule in Ireland. When similar pressure was mounted to secure a change in parliamentary representation, Wellington refused to repeat his previous act of compromise and he resigned in 1830, making way for a Whig ministry, the first since the fall of Lord Grenville in 1807, under Earl Grey.

Honoria's name, rightly or wrongly, then became romantically linked with that of Sir James Graham, a 'tall and handsome' Whig Member of Parliament with the 'manner of a dandy', while Lieutenant-Colonel Sir Henry Cooke in send-

Lady Augusta Cadogan   *Lady Honoria Cadogan*

George Cadogan

ing the London news to a friend records that 'Mrs Cadogan fait du frais to dispose of her girl [presumably Augusta, then 19]. Lazarus arose blooming in comparison with her quicksilver countenance, the very atmosphere seems to render her a living barometer, but I despair of seeing her "set fair".'[9] It was time for George to take up residence in the capital and accordingly in 1830 Downhall Hall was sold to Lord William Poulett (later the 6th Duke of Cleveland) for £44,000 and the family was removed to 16, Park Lane, in sight of Apsley House, the home of the Duke of Wellington. About now, George met the eminent novelist Sir Walter Scott who presented him with a Dandie Dinmont terrier called Fen (probably after 'Fenella' of *Peveril of the Peak* written by Sir Walter in 1822), who is shown at his master's knee in a portrait painted shortly afterwards by Francis Grant.[10] George was then in his late forties and is portrayed seated, attired in morning dress with his hair fashionably combed and wearing the bleak expression that must have struck fear into the heart of many a seaman.

The year 1830 was also marked by the death of George IV and the accession of his brother the Duke of Clarence as William IV. In view of the dead monarch's unpopularity, the new King was most reluctant to have the full panoply of a coronation and only after much pressure from his ministers, including Wellington, did he agree, which was fortunate for George as his name was included in the list of peerages conferred in honour of the occasion. The list also included the name of Admiral Sir James Saumarez, an outstanding officer who had fought with distinction at Cape St Vincent and at the battle of the Nile. On the 10th September 1831 George was created Baron Oakley of Caversham in the county of Oxford,[11] and he took his seat in the House of Lords four days later. Shortly afterwards a 'Grant of Supporters' was made to him by Garter King of Arms, Sir George Naylor, depicting a lion 'rampant regardant' and a black eagle 'navally crowned' beribboned with the Cross of the Order of Maria Theresa which, together with the Cadogan family shield, comprised his new coat of arms.[12] Lord Oakley had been appointed extra Naval aide-de-camp to the King only the year before and had evidently found royal favour. They certainly had common ground, which they might discuss when an opportune moment arose, for the King had joined the Navy as a midshipman in 1779 when he was fourteen years old.

CHAPTER XI

138, Piccadilly

Lord Oakley enjoyed his barony for only fifteen months before he succeeded to the earldom and the viscountcy upon the
death of Lord Cadogan in his eighty-fourth year, two days
before Christmas Day 1832. The 3rd Earl Cadogan was forty-
nine and his eldest son, Henry, who earlier in the year had
been awarded a first, when he took his degree at Oriel College, Oxford, assumed the courtesy title, Viscount Chelsea. In
his Will, signed in 1783 at Caversham, the late Earl Cadogan
had left all his personal estate to his brother William with a
final remainder 'unto and between all the Children of my
father'.[1] William had died many years before and accordingly
the new Lord Cadogan and his three sisters and brother would
now divide between them the sum of £94,532.11s.2d.[2] Lord
Cadogan also inherited the other moiety of the Chelsea estate,
and accordingly he was now the sole Lord of the Manor. The
2nd Earl Cadogan was, on the 3rd January 1833, the first
member of his family to be interred in a new vault in the
Chelsea Parish church of St Luke's, consecrated eight years
earlier. Before the month was out, Lord Cadogan's old commander, Lord Exmouth, died at Teignmouth; 'The booming
of the guns at Plymouth marked the passing of a great captain'. As one distinguished service career came to an end
another began: Lord Cadogan's son George received an ensign's commission in the 1st Foot Guards, an event which, in
view of his provision relating to Edward Cadogan in his will,
would presumably have appalled the 1st Earl Cadogan.

In recognition of his accession to the earldom Lord Cadogan
acquired the lease of a splendidly appointed brick-built man-

sion house at 138 Piccadilly, the upper rooms of which looked onto Green Park and the gardens of Buckingham Palace.[3] It was formerly the home of the 4th Duke of Queensberry ('a nobleman of dissipated habits' known as 'Old Q') and Lord Cadogan considerably refashioned the interior by the addition of marble chimney pieces and a carved boiserie representing the *Fables* of La Fontaine. The house was built in 1759 on five levels connected by a grand stone staircase with an ornamental iron balustrade. There were ornate cornices, ceiling panels, and massive chandeliers, and the walls displayed the paintings that once graced Caversham Lodge. The house provided a culinary department in the basement, servants' bedrooms on the top floor and eleven main rooms which were quite sufficient accommodation, as only Lady Augusta and Lady Honoria lived permanently at home now; Frederick had followed in the footsteps of the very 1st Earl Cadogan and he was boarding at Westminster School.

Lord Chelsea had entered the diplomatic service and in 1834 he was Attaché at St Petersburg. Before setting out for Russia he had entered into an affectionate relationship with his cousin, Mary Wellesley, one of Lady Emily's daughters, and evidently the months of separation only heightened their feelings for each other. Accordingly, in the spring of 1835 he sought his father's consent to their marriage. This had the effect of a broadside upon Lord Cadogan for he was only too well aware of the matrimonial shortcomings of Lady Emily, Lady Anglesey and their mother which, as far as he could judge, might well become evident in Mary Wellesley. He wrote to Lord Chelsea:

May 27 1835

MY DEAR HENRY,
It is in vain, I reflect, that I keep you longer in suspense. The strength of my objections, obscured as they have partially been by the painful circumstances which have intervened, now returns to my mind with augmented force and prescribes the only line of conduct which, for the reasons set forth in my last letter, I am

bound immutably to adopt. It would only be deceiving you were I to hold forth a hope that I ever can give my consent to your marriage with Mary Wellesley. I cannot in justice to myself accept the responsibility you have offered me, and must leave you therefore Master of your own actions and arbiter of your future fate. From this moment I am determined to interfere no more. Be your decision what it may, I can only say that in me you will find a lenient Judge, ready as far as I consistently can to promote the peace and happiness of those who have shown so little regard or mercy for my own. Believe me when I assure you that in requesting you will not reply to this letter I am actuated by kind and prudential notions alone. Our hearts and dispositions have naturally but few sympathies and, weakened as those now are by our relative positions, I dread lest anything which may fall from you should make impressions I have neither health or nerve to encounter.

I remain, Your affectionate father
CADOGAN[4]

I send a copy of this to Mary Wellesley by this day's Post.

The matter simmered on for the rest of that year with both father and son fervently hoping the other would yield. It must have been a bitter pill for Lord Cadogan, schooled in the iron discipline of the Royal Navy, to be defied by his heir in such a fundamental concern. Lady Cadogan took her worries to Paris for the season and chanced to meet Lord Anglesey who wrote to his wife that he had:

seen Ld Granville & Ld Hatherton & Edward Ellice & Greville & *Old Sugarloaf* & I know not who besides, & all the Ladies have announced their intended visits to me. I saw too Ly Cadogan & Ly Kenmare. In short London is in Paris ... Greville has been very active in getting us apartments. They are not brilliant, but they are clean. I wish you could come here per *Balloon*. Of course this will be practicable in a few years – Yet hardly in our time.... . Is there nobody here to write you all the gossip of Paris? You know how unequal I am to it. Ly Cadogan did not cease for half an hour to tell me of *their* miseries about a projected marriage. I tried to guess who the Parties were, & beat about the bush, but to no purpose. At length it came out that Ld Chelsea & Miss Wellesley were the Per-

[157]

sons, & I was compelled to acknowledge that I had never heard one syllable of the matter, nor of the young Lady's former attachment to Lord Graves which she detailed to me. All of which ignorance, or (as she probably thought) stupidity, seemed to fill her with amazement.[5]

Since her father had removed to Durham in 1827, Mary Wellesley had formed a friendship with the Marchioness of Londonderry whose husband was the half-brother of the late Foreign Secretary, Castlereagh, and owner of an extensive estate there. Lady Londonderry had subsequently befriended Lord Chelsea and accordingly Lady Cadogan then addressed a long rambling appeal to her, writing from the Hotel Meurice:

You are the only person who can do any good. Your influence over Henry is immense and I cannot therefore help appealing to you and entreating you to use it in persuading him to change his course with his Father for his own sake and for Mary's. Poor Boy he has entirely lost his Head and he writes letters which really look like the composition of the worst enemy to his cause . . .

. . . In short his last 3 letters have entirely turned the course of the tide which was setting in his favour . . . He insists on immediate consent and that he will proceed to extremities and that Mary's health admits of no delay . . . Believe me dear Lady Londonderry . . . nothing can be done until Henry comes away either to his Family or anywhere out of the neighbourhood. I believe his Father will be content with that simple expression of repentence for the language he has used. Then Lord Cadogan will concede how much I cannot say . . . I fear I have not made my meaning clear. It is so hard to write well when one feels strongly. Lord Cadogan is very ill indeed, worried into a nervous attack and we are all miserable as words can say . . . Pray, Pray do not betray me to Lord Cadogan as writing to you. I am betraying him in part by what I tell you.[6]

There was nothing that Lady Londonderry could, or perhaps would, do:

January

MY DEAR LADY CADOGAN,
I have just received your letter and I assure you I really regret your

Lady Londonderry

anxiety and unhappiness, the more so as I can do nothing to alleviate it. Lord Chelsea is not with me. Dr Wellesley, I believe, has yielded to the advice of his friends and consideration for his daughter's happiness and has allowed him to come to Bishop Wearmouth. Lord Chelsea has spent since his return from London two or three unhappy weeks here and has talked to me fully and frequently but I must add I never heard him express himself in other than terms of affection and respect to you and his Father at the same time that his purpose seemed as irrevocable as his attachment was strong.

My affection for Mary, my long knowledge of and my friendship for her makes me, I own, sanguine as to the ultimate happiness of the union, though I can perfectly understand objections that may be most natural and that the affection and anxiety of parents might point to a more ambitious choice for their oldest son. As far as I can understand, your present desire is that they should wait and really I never heard this objected to. I have not seen Mary for a month and I have never had any communication with Dr Wellesley on the subject, but in my conversation with Lord Chelsea he appeared resigned to wait patiently if hopes were given of an ultimate consent but your letters and his Father's breathed irrevocable opposition . . . What passed between Lord Chelsea and his father in London I know not and you feel it is always very difficult to pronounce between conflicting statements and correspondence perhaps partially developed. It remains only for me to add that when Lord Chelsea returned having taken his determination which I could neither alter or influence it was impossible this house should not be open to him. I endeavoured to show him all the kindness and friendship in my power under his unhappiness.[7]

There was no assistance to be found from the Duke of Wellington either:

London 21st May 1836

MY DEAR LADY CADOGAN,
I received last night your note of yesterday evening and I am very sorry that I cannot call upon you this morning as I am going out of town, not to return till Tuesday.

It appears from your note of yesterday that I had been mistaken respecting Lord Cadogan's objection to the marriage. It is in fact to the conduct of the mother that the objection is. Setting aside for a moment the virtue of this objection to the daughter who was a child when separated from the mother and who never can have felt other than aggravated evil from the mother's conduct, it could never be expected from Gerald that he should be a consenting party to a sentence against his daughter upon such grounds and still less that I should be the person to endeavour to reconcile him to make an objection.

I confess therefore that I am not sorry that circumstances prevent me from waiting upon you.

I should be most happy to give every assistance in my power to reconcile those who ought never to have had a difference and to overcome difficulties. But I cannot be a party to an objection which is essentially unjust and if once admitted must be considered conclusive upon all occasions and in all cases. Believe me Ever

Yours most sincerely,
WELLINGTON.[8]

Parental consent remained unforthcoming and in early July, Lord Chelsea obtained a special licence for the marriage. He wrote to Lady Londonderry shortly before his wedding:

Durham, Saturday.

DEAR LADY LONDONDERRY,

The veil is beyond beautiful. It has given general satisfaction and Mary is fully alive to its merits. I do so wish you could be here on Tuesday to see her wear it. It is too hard upon you to have had all the bother and none of the fun. I had no idea till I saw all the things and heard Mary's account, what trouble you had given yourself.

Mr Spence came over here and told us that he had heard from you about Seaham (Hall). He has very good naturedly undertaken to get us supplied with all we want.

I hear that my people are more abusive than ever. I am fit to be tied especially as I am not allowed to write a piece as I should wish telling them a bit of my mind. Such a system of deceit and falsehood never was known. I have sent you a copy of my father's letter which I hope you will show to any people who bother you or repeat his story. What business can he have or what excuses can he find for going on after all the declarations, just as if things remained as they

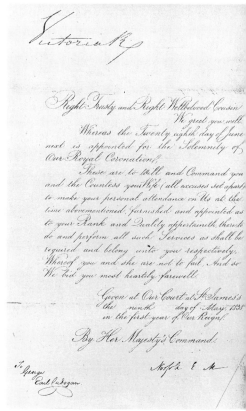

Lord Chelsea in 1864, when he had become 4th Earl Cadogan

Commanded to the Coronation

were two months ago? In addition to the letter I enclose, he wrote to Mrs Quinton soon after saying that 'he would confine himself to a religious silence on any steps his son and her sister might take.' These are his own words and let him get out of them as he can.

Nothing has happened since these letters were written except that I stayed away one month from the North when I need not have done it. I don't know why I go a twaddling as you know all about it already. What are you going to do with yourself? Do tell us so that if we happen to be going your way we may contrive to fall in with you somewhere. Many many thanks for your kind wishes. I have nothing to give you in return except a great lump of cake which I hope you will receive on Thursday morning.

God bless you and believe me ever most sincerely yours,

CHELSEA.[9]

138, Piccadilly

It was left for Mary's father to report on the wedding:

Durham 13th July 1836

MY DEAR LADY LONDONDERRY,

I do not know whether I am on my head or my feet but I must write to you one line before the post goes out to tell you that the marriage is over. The ceremony took place at 6 o'clock this evening in the Cathedral. Any thing looking so lovely as Mary did I cannot describe to you. She was quite composed and pale so that she looked like a marble thing under the veil. There was not a soul present belonging to us. To say what I would have given that you could have been here and have seen the conclusion of a business in which you have taken such an interest though it was but a melancholy [illegible]. I am sure you would have liked to see your own pet [illegible] looking so fresh and beautiful as if she had been just created. She has been so happy lately that she has grown quite fat and is very different from what she was when you last saw her. The marriage was to have taken place yesterday but Henry was unfortunately taken ill the day before and it was obliged to be deferred. They have just started for Seaham where I have no doubt they will be greeted by Spence.

I wish I could give you any details that would interest you, but I daresay they will write to you themselves very soon. I feel very desolate and wretched and you are the only person I can write to because you are almost the only person in the world who takes an equal interest with myself in this marriage. I do love you so very very much for it.

God bless you dear Lady Londonderry,

Believe me Yours very affectionately,

GERALD WELLESLEY.[10]

In addition to his continuing interest in the development of his Chelsea Estate, Lord Cadogan was also a member of the Board of Trustees, as a Sloane Family Trustee, of the British Museum and an elected member of the Trustees' Standing Committee. Sir Hans Sloane's extensive and varied collections, including 50,000 books and 32,000 medals and coins, were purchased for the nation in 1753 and formed one of the three founding collections for the Museum. This entitled two of Sloane's descendants to be trustees in perpetuity. The Trustees also included ex officio some of the most influential men in the country, such as the Archbishop of Canterbury, the Lord High Chancellor, the Speaker of the House of Commons, the First Lord of the Admiralty and the Master of the Rolls. Lord Cadogan proved an active Trustee and for some years he was a Fellow of the Society of Antiquaries, reflecting an interest that he pursued during his visits to Italy.

King William died on the 20th June 1837 and his niece Victoria, then eighteen years old, came to the throne. Lord Cadogan was duly appointed her Naval aide-de-camp and in the following year on the 28th June he took his place among his fellow peers, some of whom had brought in hampers for sustenance, to witness the coronation at Westminster Abbey. Behind them sat members of foreign royal families, the Kings and Princes in splendid uniforms, their ladies covered in diamonds. The sombre walls of the Abbey were draped with red cloth caught in scalloped borders of bright buttercup which provided an effect of 'an opera house given over to the antics of an audience at a music hall'. The chattering congregation took it upon themselves to applaud as the likes of the Duke of Wellington, his old adversary Marshal Soult, and the Prime Minister Lord Melbourne appeared. The five-hour ceremony was made the more strenuous for the Queen by her 'remarkably maladroit' clergymen: the Archbishop of Canterbury misplaced the orb, the ruby coronation ring was too small and had to be forced upon the royal finger and the Bishop of Bath and Wells missed two pages of the Order of Service – an omission that had to be made good by recalling the Queen from her retreat into St Edward's Chapel.[11] Lord Cadogan was assuredly relieved to return to the ordered calm of Piccadilly for a restoring glass. Lady Cadogan, however, was concerned about her wardrobe and the following morning she sent an urgent plea to 10, Downing Street:

138, Piccadilly

MY DEAR LORD MELBOURNE,

I am sorry to have to bother you with my toilette concerns, but I am in a scrape out of which you can get me I imagine. They bid me send the letter to a Lord of the Treasury so I suppose the first is the best.

Little Graham 'croyant bien faire' sent me a gown and cap with Palmella's things by way of safety and expedition.

The Custom House finding this with my name imagine it was an attempt at smuggling which certainly never entered my head – on this occasion at least. As you will see by the letter, I fully intended paying the duty as I constantly do for things they send me from Paris.

I assure you I had no dishonest intention, neither had Pauline – so pray get me my gown or else how am I to go to the Palace on Monday?

Believe me

Most truly yours   H. CADOGAN[12]

The Duke de Palmella can bear witness for me that no smuggling was intended, by the fact of my name and address being on the case.

All to no avail however:

Downing Street
June 29 1838

DEAR LADY CADOGAN,

Lord Melbourne desires me to me to write and tell you that he has brought the affair of your gown before the Board of Treasury, by whom it has been considered with every disposition to make an exception in your case but it is found impossible to do so without establishing a precedent which might hereafter prove most inconvenient.

So many cases are likely to occur of either friends or servants passing their goods among the baggage of Ambassadors that it is necessary to be very rigid upon this point.

Lord Melbourne is sorry that this inconvenience has been occasioned to you by the indiscretion of your friends and still more so that it cannot be remedied.

Believe me to be,

Most faithfully yours,   W. COUPER[13]

[165]

Trafalgar Square had been for some years the possible setting for a naval monument at the centre of which was to stand a statue of William IV; when the King died, however, the idea was gently put to one side. Fortuitously, perhaps, and certainly a little belatedly, three months before Victoria's coronation, the Nelson Memorial Committee held its first meeting at the Thatched House Tavern in St James's Street where, in 1800, the question of the 2nd Earl Cadogan's sanity had been discussed. A resolution proposed by Admiral Sir Pulteney Malcomb and seconded by the man who was with Nelson when he died, Vice-Admiral Sir Thomas Hardy, was passed: 'That at this meeting, impressed by and with the deepest veneration for the Memory of Lord Nelson, propose that a General Subscription be raised for the purpose of erecting a National Monument in a conspicuous part of this Metropolis in commemoration of his glorious achievements.' A temporary committee was formed with a view to: 'receiving subscriptions and communicating with Noblemen and Gentlemen with the view of forming a Permanent Committee'.

Within three weeks the Secretary was able to report that the Prime Minister, the Chancellor of the Exchequer and eighteen other 'Noblemen and Gentlemen', including Lord Cadogan, had agreed to serve on a permanent committee and shortly thereafter a large general gathering, mostly of naval captains and admirals, concluded that: 'this meeting most earnestly request the committee to make every possible endeavour to obtain a space of ground in Trafalgar Square as the site of the proposed Monument, and they cannot but express their hope that the Government will not refuse so appropriate a situation.' There followed another, larger, general meeting at which the Duke of Wellington appeared and was elected Chairman. The Secretary then read a letter from the Chancellor of the Exchequer, Thomas Spring Rice, about the use of Trafalgar Square: 'His Majesty's Government have for a considerable length of time been desirous that the site should be appropriate for the Nelson Monument, there will be therefore every willingness that a suitable site should be appropriated for this purpose, provided that the plans and designs be first approved by His Majesty's Government.' The committee thereupon arranged for the insertion of an advertisement in the national press:

The Committee for erecting a Monument to the Memory of Lord Nelson hereby give notice that they are desirous of receiving from Architects, Artists or other persons, Designs for such a Monument in Trafalgar Square.

The Committee cannot in the present state of the subscriptions fix definitely the sum to be expended, but they recommend that the estimated cost of the several Designs should be confined with the sums of £20,000 and £30,000. This condition and that of the intended site are the only restrictions to which the artists are limited.

The Committee is not bound to adopt any of the offered Designs; but rewards of £200, £150 and £100 will be given to 1st, 2nd and 3rd places ... The Designs, sealed and marked within and without with the Designer's name or any mark ... and an Estimate of the cost as accurate as he may be able to make.[14]

The response was enthusiastic and a small sub-committee of fourteen members, including Lord Cadogan, Sir Robert Peel and Spring Rice, under the chairmanship of Wellington, was set up to tackle the daunting task of assessing the merits or otherwise of 40 models and 124 designs. Eventually the design by William Railton was selected which provided for a statue of the great sailor atop a fluted column of Devon granite, rising from a square pedestal with bronze bas-relief panels depicting the Battle of St Vincent, the Battle of the Nile, the Bombardment of Copenhagen and the Death of Nelson. Work was begun on the concrete foundations in 1839 and the statue by Edward Hodges Bailey was raised in November 1843. Aptly, the bronze panels were cast from guns captured at Trafalgar and at the battles portrayed. It was generally held that the sub-committee had made a fitting choice.

Lady Emily was not destined to see the imposing memorial to her distant cousin completed as she died in December 1839

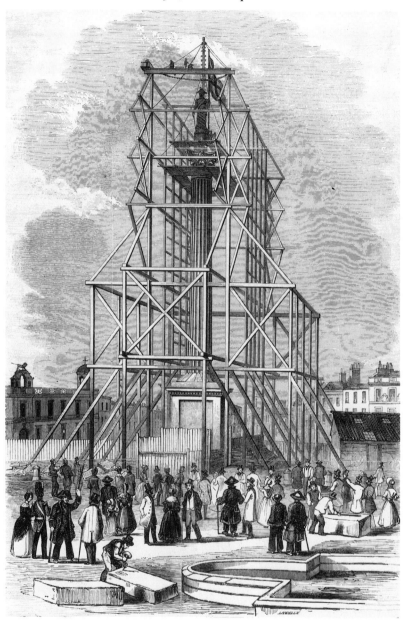

Nelson's Column under construction

at Boulogne, seemingly unreconciled either to husband or children; her body was brought back to England and buried at St Luke's. This evidence of mortality appears to have spurred Lady Louisa at last to find herself a husband and in April 1840, at the age of 52, she married the Reverend William Marsh, the 64-year old incumbent of St Mary's, Leamington of whom it was remarked that 'Few men preached a greater number of sermons'.[15] There was occasion for further celebration a few weeks later when Lady Chelsea presented her husband with a son and heir, George Henry, who was born at Durham. Lord Chelsea had now decided to enter politics and in the General Election of 1841 he was one of two Conservative members returned for Reading to support the new Conservative-Tory Prime Minister, Sir Robert Peel (Queen Victoria's bête noire) who had enjoyed a very brief period in office prior to the now deposed Whig, Lord Melbourne. Peel was in favour of free trade and accordingly import duties under his ministry were reduced which had a depressing effect on government revenue. To make good the loss he re-imposed a tax on incomes; a measure supported by Lord Chelsea but not perhaps by his father.

Lord Cadogan's name had, over the past twenty-seven years, gradually ascended the navy list and on the 23rd November 1841 he was promoted to flag rank as Rear Admiral of the Blue. An elaborate hierarchy of flag ranks had developed over the years based on the three main squadrons – the Red, White and Blue – into which fleets were organised. These squadrons were themselves further divided into the front (van), the middle (or centre) and rear divisions. An admiral commanded each squadron with junior-ranking admirals – rear and vice – also wearing their flags in each Squadron. The most senior officer was the Admiral of the Red and he ranked below the Admiral of the Fleet. The new admiral did not spend all his time in London as evidenced by a letter from Lady Granville in Rome to the Duke of Devonshire in December 1842:

Lord Cadogan appointed Admiral in Her Majesty's Fleet

The Cadogans are coming to the Palazzo Chigi, [on the Via de Corso], immense and the aspect full south, but comfortless as to want of fireplaces and *dégagements*. In short, the complaints of others make us still more satisfied with ourselves.

But here comes Frederick Cadogan, the songster, and Lady Acton with Monsieur Spada in her hand, and I must bid you good night.

[Later] Fullerton and I are going to hunt for ivy with yellow buds, to be found between Cecilia Metella's tomb and the bridge of Nomentana, supposed to have been brought from Greece by Adrian. The only representation of it is in a mosaic at the Vatican, the pendant of Pliny's doves, where there are two masks, one crowned with ivy with yellow buds. A pleasant little *chasse*. The said Mr. Fullerton is on the point of yielding to Lord Cadogan's earnest solicitations to go partners with him in the purchase of a bit of land at Tarquinia or Faleria, where they are to dig and share what they find. We think it will be awful when the moment comes of dividing the spoils – to whom the jug, to whom the arm.[16]

Lady Cadogan was an inveterate traveller and it was during a visit to the spa at Wiesbaden that she suddenly died in September 1845; she too was brought home for interment in the family vault at St Luke's. Only two years earlier, Lady Louisa had also died and before long the two Wellesley brothers, Henry and Gerald, were also gone. Mary Churchill's 'beloved child' Edward died in 1851, his marriage having proved childless.

There were other, happier, events. Frederick 'the songster' was called to the bar while George, still with the 1st Foot, was now a lieutenant-colonel. In a distribution of the General Naval Medal, Lord Cadogan received his with three clasps for the capture of the *Virginie*, the action with the *Droits de l'Homme* and the cutting out of *La Guepe*; all now so long ago. There was a further intermingling of the Cadogan and Paget lines in November 1851 when Frederick married his cousin, Lady Adelaide youngest daughter of Lord and Lady Anglesey, and in the following July Lord Chelsea, having lost his seat in Reading in 1847, was returned to Parliament as the Conservative member for Dover.

The Duke of Wellington died in 1852 followed by Lady Anglesey the year after and then Lord Anglesey. The two runaways had enjoyed a long and happy marriage notwithstanding the inauspicious beginning. Lady Anglesey had written a very reflective letter to Lord Anglesey some while earlier:

We have both been mercifully preserved through a length of years beyond the usual allotment to man, & I sincerely hope that you may still be spared for the sake of many to whom your existence is of so much importance! My own life is of little use to any Body – but time *must* be short for us both, & life fast dying away, & our latter days can *only be valuable* to ourselves as giving us a longer period for

[171]

preparation to meet our Heavenly Father ... It is a solemn subject for *us* to reflect upon *by-gone days*, past to us as if they had never been, but not so with God; in his memory every sin is recorded, and to him we must ere long give an account of all our deeds as if he were in ignorance – This we are distinctly told in his holy word, but in that blessed Book we are as clearly promised *perfect forgiveness* if we approach him deeply humbled under a sense of our sins – I feel certain that you go with me now in these things, altho' we may differ upon more trifling points our hopes and dependance rest entirely in our Saviour; without his mediation & death, what would have become of *us*? –

If it should please God to take me first I am sure that my dying moments will be soothed by the reflexions which your *present* state of mind affords me, & I pray God that you may go on daily advancing in holiness, for there is need of improvement in all of us! We have all the same means given by which *alone* we can be carried

Lord Cadogan in 1860

forward, & in the end obtain what we ask for – the Kingdom of Heaven – *There* I trust my dearest that we shall be re-united, joined by all our dear Children *yours & mine.*

I beg of you to allow My Burial to be as quiet as possible but *take care that I am really dead* beforehand – The less expence the better pleased I should be, & therefore let me be peacefully & *quietly* deposited wherever I may happen to die.

Once more God bless you![17]

Lord Cadogan was now the last of Mary Churchill's children. Ten years remained to him and he spent them at his home in Piccadilly in the care of Lady Augusta and Lady Honoria, both now past any thoughts of matrimony, occasionally meeting a few old naval cronies to talk about the days when the Navy was a man's life – before the arrival of the 'ironclad'. If his conversation had been recorded it probably would have been to the effect that, yes, he had ordered many a flogging but there was a war to be won. On reflection, he had no regrets: he had done his duty as best he might. He no doubt gained much quiet satisfaction from the manner in which his sons had matured. George had attained his colonelcy and had fought with distinction during the Crimean War at the battles of Alma, Balaklava and Inkerman. Frederick was doing well at the Bar and would no doubt in due time enter Parliament. As for Lord Chelsea, well, he looked at his will which had recently been drawn-up:

I declare that the distribution of my property hereby made as regards my children is so made from a desire to provide as well as my means enable me for those who stand most in need of my assistance and not from any want of affection for those to whom only remembrances of me are hereby given and I give to my son Lord Chelsea as a remembrance of me the legacy of nineteen guineas for a ring and I give a like legacy of nineteen guineas for a like purpose to his wife Lady Chelsea.

Lord Cadogan, Admiral of the Red and the third senior admiral in the Navy, died 'at an early hour' on Friday the 15th September 1864.

Genealogical Tables

THE CADOGAN FAMILY

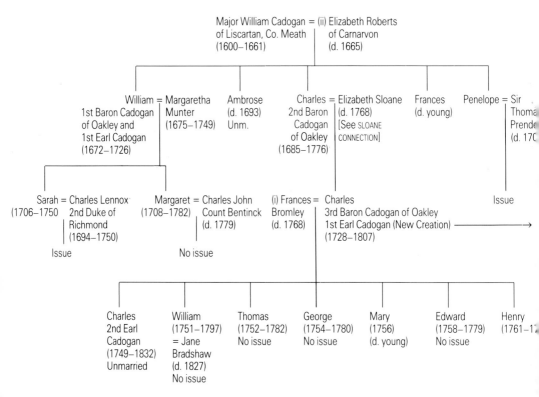

Major William Cadogan = (ii) Elizabeth Roberts
of Liscartan, Co. Meath | of Carnarvon
(1600–1661) | (d. 1665)

- William = Margaretha
  1st Baron Cadogan | Munter
  of Oakley and | (1675–1749)
  1st Earl Cadogan
  (1672–1726)

- Ambrose
  (d. 1693)
  Unm.

- Charles = Elizabeth Sloane
  2nd Baron | (d. 1768)
  Cadogan | [See SLOANE
  of Oakley | CONNECTION]
  (1685–1776)

- Frances
  (d. young)

- Penelope = Sir
  Thoma
  Prende
  (d. 17C

Sarah = Charles Lennox
(1706–1750) 2nd Duke of
Richmond
(1694–1750)

Issue

Margaret = Charles John
(1708–1782) Count Bentinck
(d. 1779)

No issue

(i) Frances = Charles
Bromley 3rd Baron Cadogan of Oakley
(d. 1768) 1st Earl Cadogan (New Creation) ——————→
(1728–1807)

Issue

- Charles
  2nd Earl
  Cadogan
  (1749–1832)
  Unmarried

- William
  (1751–1797)
  = Jane
  Bradshaw
  (d. 1827)
  No issue

- Thomas
  (1752–1782)
  No issue

- George
  (1754–1780)
  No issue

- Mary
  (1756)
  (d. young)

- Edward
  (1758–1779)
  No issue

- Henry
  (1761–1?

[176]

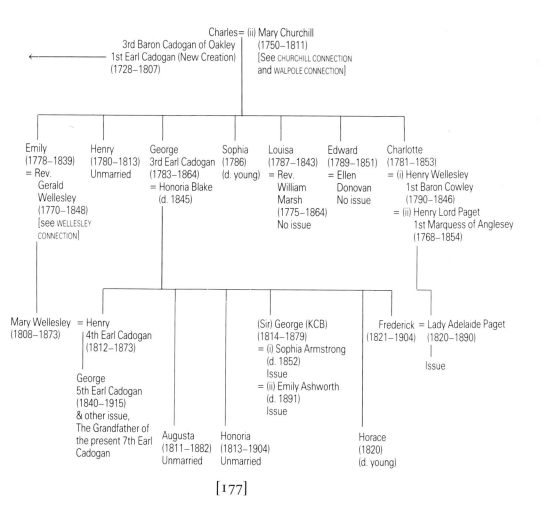

Charles = (ii) Mary Churchill
3rd Baron Cadogan of Oakley   (1750–1811)
1st Earl Cadogan (New Creation)   [See CHURCHILL CONNECTION
(1728–1807)   and WALPOLE CONNECTION]

Emily
(1778–1839)
= Rev.
  Gerald
  Wellesley
  (1770–1848)
[see WELLESLEY
CONNECTION]

Henry
(1780–1813)
Unmarried

George
3rd Earl Cadogan
(1783–1864)
= Honoria Blake
  (d. 1845)

Sophia
(1786)
(d. young)

Louisa
(1787–1843)
= Rev.
  William
  Marsh
  (1775–1864)
  No issue

Edward
(1789–1851)
= Ellen
  Donovan
  No issue

Charlotte
(1781–1853)
= (i) Henry Wellesley
     1st Baron Cowley
     (1790–1846)
= (ii) Henry Lord Paget
      1st Marquess of Anglesey
      (1768–1854)

Mary Wellesley
(1808–1873)

= Henry
  4th Earl Cadogan
  (1812–1873)

George
5th Earl Cadogan
(1840–1915)
& other issue,
The Grandfather of
the present 7th Earl
Cadogan

Augusta
(1811–1882)
Unmarried

Honoria
(1813–1904)
Unmarried

(Sir) George (KCB)
(1814–1879)
= (i) Sophia Armstrong
     (d. 1852)
     Issue
= (ii) Emily Ashworth
      (d. 1891)
      Issue

Horace
(1820)
(d. young)

Frederick
(1821–1904)

= Lady Adelaide Paget
  (1820–1890)

Issue

THE WALPOLE CONNECTION

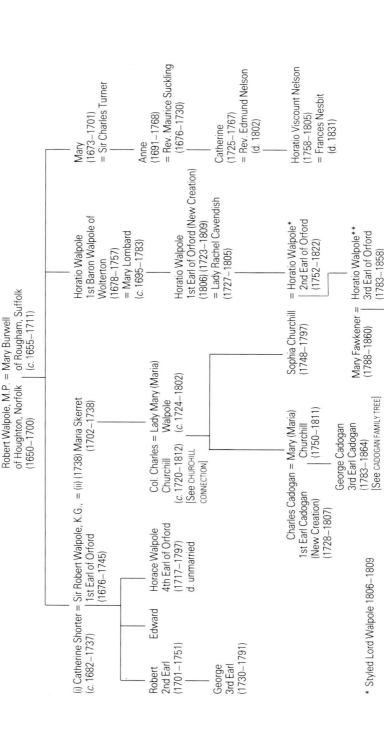

Robert Walpole, M.P. = Mary Burwell
of Houghton, Norfolk   of Rougham, Suffolk
(1650–1700)   (c. 1655–1711)

(i) Catherine Shorter = Sir Robert Walpole, K.G., = (ii) (1738) Maria Skerret
(c. 1682–1737)   1st Earl of Orford   (1702–1738)
                  (1676–1745)

Robert
2nd Earl
(1701–1751)

Edward

Horace Walpole
4th Earl of Orford
(1717–1797)
d. unmarried

George
3rd Earl
(1730–1791)

Col. Charles = Lady Mary (Maria)
Churchill   Walpole
(c. 1720–1812)   (c. 1724–1802)
[See CHURCHILL
CONNECTION]

Horatio Walpole
1st Baron Walpole of
Wolterton
(1678–1757)
= Mary Lombard
(c. 1695–1783)

Horatio Walpole
1st Earl of Orford (New Creation)
(1806) (1723–1809)
= Lady Rachel Cavendish
(1727–1805)

Charles Cadogan = Mary (Maria)
1st Earl Cadogan   Churchill
(New Creation)   (1750–1811)
(1728–1807)

Sophia Churchill
(1748–1797)

= Horatio Walpole*
2nd Earl of Orford
(1752–1822)

George Cadogan
3rd Earl Cadogan
(1783–1864)
[See CADOGAN FAMILY TREE]

Mary (1673–1701)
= Sir Charles Turner

Anne
(1691–1768)
= Rev. Maurice Suckling
(1676–1730)

Catherine
(1725–1767)
= Rev. Edmund Nelson
(d. 1802)

Horatio Viscount Nelson
(1758–1805)
= Frances Nesbit
(d. 1831)

Mary Fawkener = Horatio Walpole**
(1788–1860)   3rd Earl of Orford
               (1783–1858)

Issue

* Styled Lord Walpole 1806–1809

** Styled Lord Walpole 1809–1822

THE CHURCHILL CONNECTION

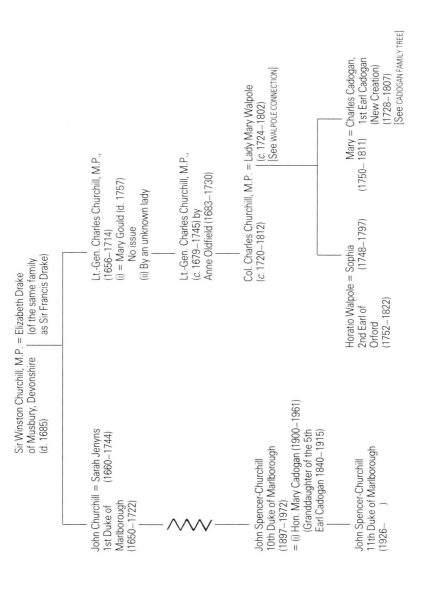

Sir Winston Churchill, M.P. = Elizabeth Drake
of Musbury, Devonshire   (of the same family
(d. 1685)   as Sir Francis Drake)

John Churchill = Sarah Jenyns
1st Duke of   (1660–1744)
Marlborough
(1650–1722)

John Spencer-Churchill
10th Duke of Marlborough
(1897–1972)
= (i) Hon. Mary Cadogan (1900–1961)
(Granddaughter of the 5th
Earl Cadogan 1840–1915)

John Spencer-Churchill
11th Duke of Marlborough
(1926–   )

Lt.-Gen. Charles Churchill, M.P.,
(1656–1714)
(i) = Mary Gould (d. 1757)
No issue
(ii) By an unknown lady

Lt.-Gen. Charles Churchill, M.P.,
(c. 1679–1745) by
Anne Oldfield (1683–1730)

Col. Charles Churchill, M.P. = Lady Mary Walpole
(c. 1720–1812)   (c. 1724–1802)
                                [See WALPOLE CONNECTION]

Horatio Walpole = Sophia   Mary = Charles Cadogan,
2nd Earl of   (1748–1797)   (1750–1811)   1st Earl Cadogan
Orford   (New Creation)
(1752–1822)   (1728–1807)
                                               [See CADOGAN FAMILY TREE]

THE SLOANE CONNECTION

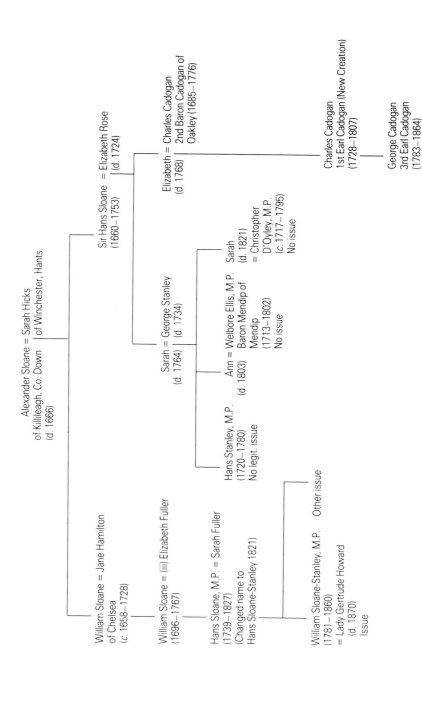

Alexander Sloane = Sarah Hicks
of Killileagh, Co. Down | of Winchester, Hants.
(d. 1666)

William Sloane = Jane Hamilton
of Chelsea
(c. 1658–1728)

William Sloane = (iii) Elizabeth Fuller
(1696–1767)

Hans Sloane, M.P. = Sarah Fuller
(1739–1827)
(Changed name to
Hans Sloane-Stanley 1821)

William Sloane-Stanley, M.P.   Other issue
(1781–1860)
= Lady Gertrude Howard
(d. 1870)
Issue

Sir Hans Sloane = Elizabeth Rose
(1660–1753) | (d. 1724)

Sarah = George Stanley
(d. 1764) | (d. 1734)

Hans Stanley, M.P.   Ann = Welbore Ellis, M.P.   Sarah
(1720–1780)   (d. 1803)   Baron Mendip of   (d. 1821)
No legit. issue   Mendip   = Christopher
                          (1713–1802)   D'Oyley, M.P.
                          No issue   (c. 1717–1795)
                                          No issue

Elizabeth = Charles Cadogan
(d. 1768) | 2nd Baron Cadogan of
            Oakley (1685–1776)

Charles Cadogan
1st Earl Cadogan (New Creation)
(1728–1807)

George Cadogan
3rd Earl Cadogan
(1783–1864)

THE WELLESLEY CONNECTION

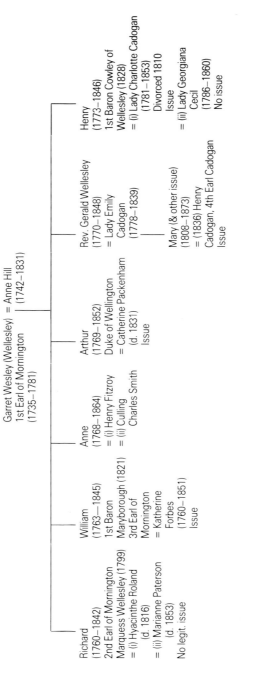

Garret Wesley (Wellesley) = Anne Hill
1st Earl of Mornington   (1742–1831)
(1735–1781)

Richard
(1760–1842)
2nd Earl of Mornington
Marquess Wellesley (1799)
= (i) Hyacinthe Roland
    (d. 1816)
= (ii) Marianne Paterson
    (d. 1853)
No legit. issue

William
(1763—1845)
1st Baron
Maryborough (1821)
3rd Earl of
Mornington
= Katherine
Forbes
(1760–1851)
Issue

Anne
(1768–1864)
= (i) Henry Fitzroy
= (ii) Culling
    Charles Smith

Arthur
(1769–1852)
Duke of Wellington
= Catherine Packenham
    (d. 1831)
Issue

Rev. Gerald Wellesley
(1770–1848)
= Lady Emily
    Cadogan
    (1778–1839)

Mary (& other issue)
(1808–1873)
= (1836) Henry
Cadogan, 4th Earl Cadogan
Issue

Henry
(1773–1846)
1st Baron Cowley of
Wellesley (1828)
= (i) Lady Charlotte Cadogan
    (1781–1853)
    Divorced 1810
    Issue
= (ii) Lady Georgiana
    Cecil
    (1786–1860)
    No issue

APPENDIX

The 3rd Earl Cadogan
Last Will & Testament

THIS IS THE LAST WILL AND TESTAMENT OF THE RIGHT HONORABLE GEORGE EARL CADOGAN I appoint my son Frederick William Cadogan and my daughters Augusta Sarah Cadogan and Honoria Louisa Cadogan my Executor and Executrixes and I declare that the distribution of my property hereby made as regards my children is so made from a desire to provide as well as my means enable me for those who stand most in need of my assistance and not from any want of affection for those to whom only remembrances of me are hereby given and I give to my son Lord Chelsea as a remembrance of me the legacy of nineteen guineas for a ring and I give a like legacy of nineteen guineas for a like purpose to his wife Lady Chelsea and I give a like legacy for a like purpose to each of my two other sons George Cadogan and Frederick William Cadogan And I give to my son Frederick William Cadogan a legacy of Two thousand pounds and to each of them my daughters Augusta Sarah and Honoria Louisa a legacy of Two thousand pounds And as regards those legacies as well as the further provision hereby made for them in the way of income I hereby declare to my daughters but without creating any trust or obligation by such declaration that should they not require in their lifetimes fully to dispose thereof or make use of the same it would be my wish that they should bear in mind that I have preferred their claims as now immediately pressing on me than those of my son Frederick William and his children but nevertheless they will be at liberty to use and dispose of all the benefits hereby given to them as they think fit And I give to Hannah Hill the confidential female domestic of my late dear Wife Honoria Louisa Countess Cadogan the sum of One thousand pounds as a very inadequate testimony of my regard and gratitude for the attachment she has always evinced towards my family during the long period she has been in my service and I also give to her my Gold Watch made by Le Roi And I give to my Steward Paul Laye Two hundred pounds and to my Valet Auguste Guinet One hundred pounds And I give to my Upper Servant Mrs. Howitt an annuity of twenty pounds to be payable to her during her life and to commence from the day of my decease and to be payable half yearly And I give to every one of my servants male or female except those above named who shall be in my service and shall have been so for five years previously to my decease one years wages over and above the wages that may be due or accruing due to them at my decease And I direct that all legacies hereby given and the said annuity of twenty pounds shall be paid free of legacy duty and the legacies shall be payable six months after my decease and bear interest from that day at four per cent per annum until paid And as to all my ESTATE AND EFFECTS whatsoever and wheresoever real or personal particularly my leasehold Mansion situate in Piccadilly I give devise and bequeath the same and every part thereof unto my son Frederick William Cadogan and my said two daughters their heirs executors administrators and assigns Upon trust that they or the survivors or survivor of them or his or her executors or administrators do and shall when and as they he or she in their his or her sole discretion shall think proper sell and dispose of all my real estate including in that description the said leasehold premises And in the meantime let set or demise the same either from year to year or for any less or longer period and at such rent and under such terms as they or he in their his or her sole judgement shall think fit or expedient And upon further trust that the said Trustees or Trustee do and shall sell and dispose of and convert into money all such part or parts of my personal estate as shall not consist of money or of stocks funds or securities for money of the description hereinafter mentioned as investments for my residuary Estate And I declare that the rents and profits or other income to accrue due from and after my decease of and from all my said trust estate from time to time remaining unsold or unconverted shall be received by my said Trustees and applied in the same manner as the annual income to arise from such estate if sold or converted and invested would be applicable by virtue of this my Will And I do hereby declare that my said Trustees or Trustee shall stand possessed of the principal monies to arise from or which shall constitute any part of my estate and effects Upon trust in the first place thereout to pay such debts as are properly payable by them out of my estate and to pay thereout also my funeral and testamentary expenses and the several legacies hereby bequeathed or which I shall give by any Codicil hereto And do and shall lay out the surplus of the monies to arise by such sale and conversion as aforesaid and of such part of my estate as shall consist of money in or upon any of the Government stocks or funds or other Government securities of the United Kingdom or upon the securities of any freehold copyhold or leasehold heriditaments and premises in England or Wales the leasehold premises being held for an unexpired term of not less than sixty years in or upon the mortgages bonds or debentures debenture stocks or other securities of any incorporated public company actually paying dividends in the names or name of the Trustees or Trustee for the time being of this my Will with power from time to time at the sole discretion of the said Trustees or Trustee to vary or transpose the stocks funds or securities in or upon which such investments should be made as occasion shall require or as shall be found convenient And I hereby declare that my said Trustees or Trustee for the time being do and shall stand and be possessed of the trust monies stocks funds and securities acquired with or constituting part of my estate including all securities of which I may die possessed and the interest dividends and annual produce thereof respectively upon and for the trusts intents and purposes following that is to say Upon trust after providing thereout for the said annuity of twenty pounds so long as that annuity shall continue payable to pay the interest and annual produce of the said trust monies stocks funds and securities to or permit the same to be received by my said two daughters or their respective assigns for and during the term of their joint natural lives in equal shares And after the decease of either Upon trust to pay the interest and annual produce thereof thenceforth to accrue due to or permit the same to be received by the survivor of my said daughters for and during the term of her natural life the income of all such stocks funds and securities nevertheless in case of the marriage of both or either of my daughters to be for the sole and separate use free from marital control And from and after the decease of both my said daughters Upon trust that my said Trustees or Trustee shall pay or transfer my said trust estate stocks monies and securities and the interest dividends and annual produce thereof unto my son Frederick William Cadogan his executors or administrators And I give to my son Frederick William Cadogan and his heirs all estates vested in me as Trustee or Mortgagee but subject to the equities affecting the same and so that any money due to me on mortgage be dealt with as part of my residuary estate Provided always and I hereby declare that if the Trustees herein named or appointed or to be appointed as hereinafter mentioned or any of them their or any of their executors or administrators be or desire to be discharged from or originally or at anytime decline or refuse or become incapable to act in the trusts hereby in them reposed as aforesaid before the said trusts shall be fully executed then and so often as the same shall happen it shall be lawful for my son Frederick William Cadogan if living but if dead for his executors or administrators for the time being by any deed or Instrument in writing to be by them or him sealed and dated in the presence of two reliable witnesses from time to time to substitute or appoint any other persons or person to be Trustees or Trustee in the place of the Trustees or Trustee dying or desiring to be discharged or declining or refusing or becoming incapable to act as aforesaid and when and so often as any Trustee shall be nominated as aforesaid all the trust estate monies and premises or such of them as shall remain subject to the trusts aforesaid shall be thereupon with all convenient speed conveyed assigned and transferred in such sort and manner and so as that the same may be effectually vested in the person or persons so to be appointed as aforesaid either solely or jointly with the surviving or remaining Trustee or Trustees as occasion shall require upon and for the trusts intents and purposes herein-before declared concerning the said trust estate monies and premises or such of them as shall be then subsisting undetermined and capable of taking effect and the person or persons so to be appointed as aforesaid shall have all the powers and authorities of the Trustee or Trustees in whose room he or they shall be substituted And I declare that the provisions contained in the Act of Parliament 23 and 24 Victoria Cap 145 relating to Wills shall be applicable to this Will except the power to appoint new Trustees given by that Act which power shall not take effect or be embodied herein or be applicable hereto In witness whereof I the said George Earl Cadogan have to this my last Will and Testament set my hand this ninth day of July One thousand eight hundred and sixty one – CADOGAN Signed and acknowledged by the said George Earl Cadogan the Testator as his last Will and Testament in the presence of us all present at the same time who at his request in his presence and in the presence of each other have subscribed our names as Witnesses hereto the alterations in the first sheet against which we have set our initials being first made – W. M. FLADGATE 40 Craven Street Strand Solicitor – GEORGE FINCH same place Solicitor

THIS IS A CODICIL to the last Will of me THE RIGHT HONOR-ABLE GEORGE EARL CADOGAN which Will bears date on or about the 9th day of July One thousand eight hundred and sixty one I give to my Granddaughter Charlotte Cadogan the oldest daughter of my son Frederick William Cadogan a legacy of five hundred pounds to be invested by my Executors for her benefit within six calendar months from my decease in such manner as the Law allows and the income to be accumulated until she shall attain the age of twenty one or be married and the Capital and accumulations to be then transferred to her but should she die under the age of twenty one and unmarried the Capital and accumulations to go to her brother the only son of my said son and her two younger sisters now living or such of them her brother and two sisters as shall attain the age of twenty one years or being females marry under age with benefit of survivorship amongst them in case of the death of any without attaining a vested interest and if but one such brother or sister live to attain a vested interest then the whole to go to such only brother or sister and the others of each to accumulate until they become transferrable and I give to Emma Bettridge the niece of Hannah Hill in my said Will named a legacy of One hundred pounds In Witness whereof I have hereunto set my hand this twenty fifth day of August in the year of our Lord One thousand eight hundred and sixty two – Cadogan – Signed and Sealed by the said George Earl Cadogan the Testator as and for a Codicil to his last Will and Testament in the presence of us being present at the same time who in his presence at his request and in the presence of each other have hereunto subscribed our names as Witnesses – W. M. FLADGATE 40 Craven Street Strand Solicitor – GEORGE FINCH same place Solicitor

PROVED at London with a Codicil 19th October 1864 by the Oath of Frederick William Cadogan Esquire commonly called The Honorable Frederick William Cadogan the Son and Augusta Sarah Cadogan commonly called Lady Augusta Sarah Cadogan a Spinster and Honoria Louisa Cadogan commonly called Lady Honoria Louisa Cadogan Spinster the daughters the Executors to whom Admon was granted.

Notes and References

FOREWORD

1 *Daily Express*, 31st March 1989, p.17.
2 A.F. Fremantle, *England in the Nineteenth Century*, Vol. II p.416.
3 Lawrence James, *Mutiny*, p.71.
4 Lawrence James, ibid, p.74.

CHAPTER I

1 Arthur Dasent, *The History of St James's Square*, p.127. Occupied by the London Library since 1845 and rebuilt 1896.
2 *Dictionary of National Biography* (hereafter DNB).
3 Madame du Deffand to Horace Walpole, 15th February and 2nd April 1771, pp.27 and 56.
4 'The envious man belittles himself'. 'Est' was added later.
5 Lady Hervey writing to Lady Mary Montagu on the 7th January 1755, *The Complete Peerage*, Vol. IX, p.133.
6 *The Letters and Journals of Lady Mary Coke*.
7 Horace Walpole, *Memoirs of the Reign of George III*. For an equivalent 1989 value of this and other money sums multiply by 45.
8 Horace Walpole, ibid. Lord Cadogan's will proved 22nd May 1807.
9 Public Record Office, Chancery Lane PROB 11/1460. Edward was probably buried in the former military cemetery at Praslin on St Lucia.
10 *Diaries of Mrs Philip Lybbe Powys 1756–1808*, pp.161–162.
11 Buried 29th July 1782 in the chapel at Raaphorst, Wassenaar, close to the Hague, in the family vault wherein already lay the 1st Earl Cadogan's wife Margaretha (née Munter), interred 7th November 1749.
12 The 1st Earl Cadogan's granddaughter (1745–1826) who according to Horace Walpole was 'more beautiful than you can conceive'. Lady Sarah was presented at Court in 1759 where the future George III fell in love with her and expressed a hope of 'raising her to a Throne'. His mother, however, opposed the union and the young lady who might otherwise have become Queen (George II died the following year) married firstly Sir Charles Bunbury and then, in

1781, George Napier by whom she had five sons and three daughters. 'Very few families, at any time, have produced sons of such talent and distinction.' Charles, George and William Napier were three of Wellington's most famous officers.

13 *Biographical Index to the House of Lords*, 1808. Estimated sale price £100,000 per 'Twelve Lordships since the Conquest' by G.L-W. Mackenzie, Ch.XI.Ms. Berkshire County Library. Major Marsac (1736–1820) was a former officer in the East India Company army and a natural grandson of George I. Buried at Caversham.

14 Mrs Powys, ibid, pp.213–214.

15 *Ipswich Journal*, 4th April 1778.

16 An engraving survives but the whereabouts of the portrait are a mystery. The 1st Earl Cadogan (of the new creation) may have disposed of it following subsequent events. Reynolds was paid £78.15s., for his services.

17 E.B. Chancellor, *The Squares of London*, p.66. The house was subsequently re-numbered 23 and demolished *c.* 1927.

18 Le Neve's *Fasti* for Rochester, p.66.

19 It seems likely that George followed his brother Henry to Eton College, although his name is not shown on the School Lists. These, however, are not definitive.

20 The Marquess of Anglesey, *One-Leg*, p.23.

CHAPTER II

1 Edward Osler, *The life of Admiral Viscount Exmouth*, p.165.

2 N.A.M. Rodger, *The Wooden World*, p.275.

3 Captain Frederic Chamier, R.N., *The Life of a Sailor*, pp.19–24.

4 C. Northcote Parkinson, *Edward Pellew*, p.133. Letter dated 18th February 1796.

5 Parkinson, ibid, pp.134–135.

6 Parkinson, ibid, p.137.

7 Parkinson, ibid, pp.147–149.

8 37 Geo. III No. 116.

CHAPTER III

1 Parkinson, ibid, pp.175–178.

2 Cutting from local contemporary newspaper (title unrecorded) in Berkshire County Library.

3 Osler, ibid, p.187.

4 Rodger, ibid, p.229.

5 Parkinson, ibid, p.208.

6 Parkinson, ibid, p.213.

7 Broken up at Sheerness 1816.

8 Parkinson, ibid, pp.220–221.
9 Dudley Pope, *Life in Nelson's Navy*, p.226.

CHAPTER IV

1 PROB 11/1529.
2 The *Impetueux* (formerly *Amerique*), 182′6″ × 48′6″, was broken-up in 1813.
3 Hart subsequently had a very full and interesting career. In 1805 he accompanied Lord Cornwallis, as Governor-General, to India where he became Flag-Lieutenant to Pellew in the 74-gun *Culloden*. He was knighted in 1836 and promoted Rear-Admiral in 1846.
4 PRO Kew ADM 6/100.
5 5th Rate, launched Chatham 18th November 1800, 1,071 b.m., 150′ × 40′6″. Up to 1873, the tonnage of a vessel is the 'builders measurement' (b.m.), a capacity arrived at by calculating the number of tuns (casks) of wine that the ship could carry. After 1873 displacement tonnage was used until 1926 when standard displacement was introduced. The *Indefatigable* was 1400 b.m.
6 *Hary-O, The Letters of Lady Harriet Cavendish*, p.42.
7 *The Diary and Correspondence of Henry Wellesley*, p.13. A translation from the French.
8 Ibid. p.13.
9 Ibid. p.14.

CHAPTER V

1 The *Leda* was wrecked near Milford Haven in 1808.
2 Launched 9th April 1796, 423 b.m., 110′ × 29′6″.
3 C.S. Forester, *The Young Hornblower*, p.341.
4 Pope, ibid, p.137.
5 *Naval Chronicle* 1805, pp.146–147.
6 Archives de France, Marine BB 4 230/232, folios 195/6 and 129.
7 Archives de France, ibid.
8 *Cyane* was recaptured off Tobago in October 1805 and renamed *Cerf*. Sold 12th January 1809.
9 Launched Dartmouth 4th January 1806, 387 b.m. Wrecked 7th January 1813 near Leith, Scotland.
10 Geoffrey Callender, *The Naval Side of British History*, p.214. Apropos Nelson's celebrated love affair, suffice it to note here that Lady Hamilton's mother Mrs Hart chose to be known as 'Mrs Cadogan' after 'an aristocratic family from the Welsh border' whence she came. Pocock, ibid, p.174.
11 Dudley Pope, *The Black Ship*, pp.141–143.
12 Lawrence James, *Mutiny*, p.72.

13 *Later Correspondence of George III*, Vol. IV, p.412.
14 Ibid.

CHAPTER VI

1 PROB 11/1460. In the event Lord Chelsea (later the 2nd Earl Cadogan) was to be interred at Chelsea.
2 *Naval Chronicle* 1806, p.258. Dispatch from Major-General Beresford to Lord Castlereagh dated 16th July 1806. The *Narcissus* (894 b.m., 142′ × 38′) became a convict ship in 1823 and was sold in January 1837.
3 Sir J.W. Fortescue, *A History of the British Army*, Vol. XIII, pp. 424–425.
4 Launched South Shields 9th April 1806. 540 b.m., 119′ × 31′6″. Broken up October 1816.
5 Sir Charles Oman, *Wellington's Army, 1809–14*. See *One-Leg*, p.81.

CHAPTER VII

1 Sir C. Webster (Ed.), *Some Letters of the Duke of Wellington to his brother, William Wellesley-Pole*, RHS, Camden Miscellany, XVIII, 1948, No's 22 and 23.
2–7 Anglesey, *One-Leg*, pp.91–96. Gerald Valerian Wellesley, jnr., was described by Lady Wellesley as 'The Wretched infant (who) is rejected by everybody'. The Duke of Wellington and his wife adopted him and he became Queen Victoria's 'much loved' Dean of Windsor (d. 1882). Elizabeth Longford, *Wellington, The Years of The Sword*, p.256.
8 Duke of Wellington's papers, University of Southampton, WP1/249/15.
9–11 *Hary-O.* pp.307–311. Sir Walter Farquhar (1738–1819) was 'a very able and successful physician' (DNB). He was the last occupant of Cadogan House in Chelsea before it was demolished (*c.* 1801) to make way for the present Duke of York's Headquarters.
12–19, 21–22 Anglesey, ibid, pp.100–112. It has been stated elsewhere that Henry Cadogan fought the duel with Paget (see Longford, ibid, p.381). It is now clear, however, that his brother George did in fact defend the family honour. Assuming that Captain M'Kenzie was a post captain in the Royal Navy, there were three such at the time of the duel, respectively Adam, George and Kenneth. Which one was George's second is unknown. Henry Cadogan's second, 'Mr Sloane', was likely to have been William Sloane (-Stanley) or one of his brothers.
20 Named Lady Emily Paget (d. 1893). Married Viscount Sydney (1805–90).

Notes and References

CHAPTER VIII

1 Duke of Wellington's papers, ibid, WP1/263/48.
2 5th Rate, launched Plymouth 17th November 1804. 667 b.m. Wrecked Firth of Forth 18th December 1810. George Cadogan was not in command at this time.
3 Longford, ibid, p.256.
4 John Marshall, *Royal Navy Biography*, p.194.
5 *Journal of a Soldier of The LXXI Regiment 1806–1815*, Constable, 1828.
6 Lt. Col. L.B. Oatts, *The Story of the Highland Light Infantry*, pp.23/24.
7 The House of Lords Record Office, George Cadogan relinquished command of the *Pallas* on 3rd May 1810 and was without a command until 6th June 1811 when he went on board the *Havannah*. Lieutenant-General Sir James Pulteney, b. 1751, commanded land forces at Ferrol in 1800 and died 26th April 1811 as the result of an accident with a powder flask. Lord P (Paget) was 'the man he [Wellington] needed. But it might make a bad impression at Cadiz to invite so soon the seducer of Henry's wife.' Longford, ibid, p. 324.
8 Sir Charles Oman, *A History of the Peninsular War* (1902), Vol. VI. The heights were eventually secured with the timely assistance of the 50th regiment and the 92nd Highlanders. The 71st lost fourteen other officers and 301 rank and file killed and wounded.
9 The House of Lords Record Office.
10 Ibid. Other more Nelsonian dying words recorded elsewhere are seemingly incorrect. See *The Cadogan Estate*, R. Pearman, Haggerston Press, 1986.
11 Private Act of Parliament 6 Geo IV–Cap 16, p.15.
12 Duke of Wellington's papers, Southampton, WP1/1232/2.

CHAPTER IX

1 *Naval Chronicle* 1811, p.340. The *Havannah* was launched at Liverpool 26th March 1811. 949 b.m., 145′ × 38′6″. Training ship 19th March 1860. Sold 1905 for break-up.
2 PROB 11/1529.
3 PROB 11/1534.
4 Anglesey, ibid, p.112.
5 *Naval Chronicle* 1813, p.238.
6 *Gentleman's Magazine* 1813, p.279.
7 *Naval Chronicle* 1813, p.76.
8 *Naval Chronicle* 1813, pp.435–436.
9 *Gentleman's Magazine* 1813, p.72.

10 Ibid, pp.267–268. Henry's death caught the public imagination and this verse was published in July 1813 (*Gentleman's Magazine*, p.63):

VITTORIA

Cadogan, wounded in the fight,
Cries, 'Bear, Oh! bear me to yon height,
That, till mine eyes can gaze no more,
And ev'ry hope of life is o'er,
I may behold the Frenchmen fly,
And hear the shouts of Victory!'
  They bore the Hero to yon height:
He saw the Frenchmen put to flight!
And when 'Huzza!' the Victors cried,
He heard them with a Soldier's pride,
Bless'd his brave Countrymen, and died!

J. MAYNE

Monuments were erected in St Paul's Cathedral, Glasgow Cathedral, St Luke's, Chelsea and St Mary's at Santon Downham. There is also a Cadogan Street in Glasgow.

11 *Naval Chronicle* 1813, pp.510–511.
12 Ibid, 1814, p.76.

CHAPTER X

1 Österreichisches Staatsarchiv – Kriegsarchiv, Wien. Franz, or Francis II, was also Holy Roman Emperor until the extinction of the Empire in 1806; as Emperor of Austria he reigned until 1835. The Imperial Military Order of Maria Theresa (1717–1780; Empress) was created on the 13th May 1757 and comprised three classes: Grand Cross, Commander and Knight. Its badge was a 'cross of eight points, of gold, enamelled white, edged with gold'. George's decoration was returned to Vienna following his death. Wellington was appointed a Grand Cross in 1814 and Anglesey a Commander the year following. The Order was last awarded in 1919. See *A Concise Account of Foreign Orders of Knighthood*, Nicholas Carlisle, 1839.
2 The House of Lords Record Office.
3 Anglesey, ibid, p.355.
4 DNB.
5 PROB 11/1063.
6 PROB 11/1651.
7 6 Geo IV – Cap 16 and Cap 17.
8 *Letters of Harriet Countess Granville*, 1810–45, Longmans, Green, & Co., 1894, p.402.
9 Duke of Wellington's papers, Southampton, WP1/1120/1.

10 Later Sir Francis Grant (1803–78) who painted a portrait of Sir Walter Scott in 1831. Grant might perhaps be the link between the novelist and George Cadogan. Elected President of the Royal Academy 1866.

11 George Cadogan does not appear to have owned land in Caversham and his choice of barony and territorial designation is most likely a simple acknowledgement of the Cadogan family's association with both Caversham (now in the Royal County of Berkshire) and Oakley in Buckinghamshire.

12 When the 1st Earl Cadogan was enobled on the 21st June 1716 the Supporters granted comprised a lion rampant regardant (looking backwards) and a dragon in similar pose; his shield bore a lion rampant regardant in the 1st and 4th quarters and three 'couped' boars' heads in the 2nd and 3rd quarters – these latter beasts were, according to legend, emblazoned on the shield carried by his Welsh ancestor Cadwgan who lived at the turn of the millennium. This composite coat of arms descended to the 2nd Baron Cadogan of Oakley and then through to the 2nd Earl Cadogan. At some time subsequent to Lord Oakley's succession to the earldom the supporters were changed and the beribboned eagle replaced the dragon, but a dragon's head remained the family crest. The eagle is thought to represent the 3rd Earl Cadogan's links with the Hapsburg Empire. See *The First Earl Cadogan* and *The Cadogan Estate*, R. Pearman, Haggerston Press, 1988, 1986.

CHAPTER XI

1   PROB 11/1818.
2   PRO/IR26/1316.
3   The house remains today although it is used commercially. The front elevation was refaced in Portland stone *c*. 1891.
4   The Londonderry Collection at Durham County Council Archive, D/Lo/C549.
5   Anglesey, ibid. Lord Graves was the eldest son of Anglesey's sister, Mary.
6   The Londonderry Collection.
7   Ibid.
8   The House of Lords Record Office.
9   The Londonderry Collection.
10 Ibid.
11 Raymond Hudson, 'Vivat Victoria', *The Lady*, 21st–27th June 1988.
12 Royal Archives, Windsor, Box 21/3.
13 Ibid.

14 PRO WORKS 6.119, Nelson Memorial Committee Minute Book 1838–44.
15 DNB.
16 *Letters of Countess Granville*, p.343. The Palazzo Chigi is now the official residence of the Italian Prime Minister.
17 Anglesey, ibid, p.333.

Bibliography

Authorities Consulted

AUSTRIA

Österreichische Nationalbibliothek, Wien; Österreichisches Staatsarchiv – Kriegsarchiv, Wien.

ENGLAND

British Museum, Cambridgeshire County Council Record Office, Canterbury Cathedral Record Office, Christie's Auctioneers, City of Westminster Archives & Local Studies Dept., College of Arms, Coutts & Co, Devon County Council Archives Dept, English Heritage, Eton College Library, Greater London Record Office & Library, Grosvenor Estate, Guildhall Library, House of Commons Public Information Office, House of Lords Records Office, Kent County Council Archives Dept, Lambeth Palace Library, London Borough of Richmond upon Thames Libraries & Arts Dept, National Army Museum, National Maritime Museum, Naval Historical Library (MOD), News International Newspapers Ltd, Oxfordshire County Council Archives Dept, Public Record Office Chancery Lane, Public Record Office Kew, Reading Public Library Local History Dept, Royal Academy of Arts, Royal Archives Windsor Castle, Royal County of Berkshire Record Office, Society of Antiquaries, Sotheby's Auctioneers, Suffolk County Council Archives Dept, University of Southampton Library.

FRANCE

Archives de France, Paris; Archives Municipales, Ville de Nancy; Musée de la Marine, Paris; Service Historique de la Marine, Vincennes.

GERMANY

Hessisches Hauptstaatsarchiv Wiesbaden.

Bibliography

HOLLAND

Gemeente Archief's-Gravenhage.

IRELAND

Office of the Chief Herald Dublin.

SCOTLAND

University of Aberdeen, Dept. of History of Art.

WEST INDIES

Direction Departementale des Services d'Archives de la Martinique, St Lucia National Trust.

Printed Sources and Works of Reference

Alumni Cantabrigienses 1752–1900; Alumni Oxonienses 1715–1886; A Naval Biographical Dictionary by William R. O'Byrne, 1849; *Burke's Genealogical and Heraldic History of the Peerage and Baronetage (and Knightage)*; *Dictionary of National Biography*; *Gentleman's Magazine*; *House of Commons 1754–90* (History of Parliament Trust); *Hodson's Index of the Officers of the East India Company and Indian Armies* (National Army Museum); *Naval Chronicles 1795–1814; Royal Navy Biography* by John Marshall, 1827; *The Complete Peerage*, 1936; *The House of Commons 1715–1754*, by Romney Sedgwick, 1949; *Who's Who of British Members of Parliament 1832–1855*.

Published Works

Anglesey, The Marquess of, *One-Leg, The Life and Letters of Henry William Paget, First Marquess of Anglesey, K.G., 1768–1854*, Jonathan Cape, 1961.

Bryan, George, *Chelsea in the Olden & Present Times*, published by the Author, 1869.

Callender, Geoffrey, *The Naval Side of British History*, Christophers, 1924.

Chamier, Captain Frederick, R.N., *The Life of a Sailor*, Richard Bentley, 1832.

Coke, Lady Mary, *The Letters and Journals of, 1756–1774*, privately published Edinburgh, 1889–96.

Colledge, J.J., *Ships of the Royal Navy*, David & Charles, 1969.

Bibliography

Dasent, Arthur Irwin, *The History of St. James's Square*, Macmillan, 1895.

Forester, C.S., *The Hornblower Companion*, Michael Joseph, 1964.

Forester, C.S., *The Young Hornblower*, Michael Joseph, 1964.

Fortescue, Sir John William, *A History of the British Army*, published 1899–1930.

Fremantle, A.F., *England in the Nineteenth Century 1801–1810*, George Allen & Unwin, 1930.

George III, *Later Correspondence of*, (1802–1807), Cambridge University Press, 1968.

Hibbert, Christopher, *The English, A Social History 1066–1945*, Paladin Books, 1988.

James, Lawrence, *Mutiny*, Buchan & Enright, 1987.

Leveson-Gower, Sir George (Ed), *Hary-O, The Letters of Lady Harriet Cavendish 1796–1809*, John Murray, 1940.

Longford, Elizabeth, *Wellington, The Years of the Sword*, Panther Books, 1985.

Mace, Rodney, *Trafalgar Square, Emblem of Empire*, Lawrence & Wishart, 1976.

Oatts, Lt.Col. L.B., *The Story of the Highland Light Infantry*, Thos. Nelson, 1952.

Osler, Edward, *The Life of Admiral Viscount Exmouth*, Smith Elder, 1835.

Parkinson, C. Northcote, *Edward Pellew, Viscount Exmouth, Admiral of the Red*, Methuen, 1934.

Petre, F. Loraine, *History of the Royal Berkshire Regiment*, 1925.

Pevsner, Sir Nikolaus, *The Buildings of England, London*, Vol. I, Penguin Books, 1985.

Pocock, Tom, *Horatio Nelson*, Cassell, 1987.

Pope, Dudley, *Life in Nelson's Navy*, Unwin Hyman, 1987.

Pope, Dudley, *The Black Ship*, Weidenfeld & Nicolson, 1963.

Powys, Mrs Philip Lybbe, *The Diaries of*, Longmans, Green, 1899.

Reese, M.M., *Goodwood's Oak, The Life and Times of the Third Duke of Richmond, Lennox and Aubigny*, Threshold Books, 1987.

Rodger, N.A.M., *The Wooden World*, Fontana Press, 1988.

Strachey, Lytton (Ed), and Roger Fulford (Ed), *The Greville Memoirs 1814–1860*, Macmillan, 1938.

Stroud, Dorothy, *Capability Brown*, Faber, 1984.

Thomas, David, A., *A Companion to the Royal Navy*, Harrap, 1988.

Walpole, Horace, *Correspondence with Madame du Deffand and Mademoiselle Sanadon*, Oxford University Press, 1939.

Walpole, Horace, *Memoirs of the Reign of George III*, (Ed.) G.F. Russell Barker, 1894.

Wellesley, Col. the Hon. F.A., (Ed)., *The Diary and Correspondence of Henry Wellesley, First Lord Cowley 1790–1846*, Hutchinson, 1930.

Acknowledgements

This volume could not have been produced without the generous help afforded by the staff of many record offices and libraries both at home and abroad. I thank them all. Specific mention must be made of the splendid Bath Reference Library where many dusty volumes of the *Naval Chronicle* and other less frequently referred-to works were tirelessly made available. I am also particularly indebted to the Marquess of Anglesey for his kind permission to quote from *One-Leg* and from the Plas Newydd Papers.

Illustration Sources

[201]

Illustration Sources

Index

Index

Index

Kulm, 141

Lacrosse, Commodore Jean Raimond, 50
Lameillerie, Captain Antoine Delamare, de, 80
Leipzig, battle of, 142
Lennox, Lady Sarah, 18
Lewis, Thomas, 64, 65
Liniers, General, 95, 121
Lisbon, 98, 115
Liverpool, Robert Jenkinson, 2nd Earl of, 118, 136, 150
Lizard Point, 45
Lloyd, William, 17
Logan, Surgeon Thomas Galbraith, 130
Londonderry, Robert Stewart, Viscount Castlereagh, 2nd Marquess of, 115, 118, 136, 140, 146, 150
Londonderry, 3rd Marquess of, 158
Londonderry, Marchioness of, 158, (159)
L'Orient, 68
Louis XVI, King of France, 25
Louis XVIII, King of France, 145
Lowestoft, 24
Luneville, the Treaty of, 1801, 69

Mackenzie, Hugh, Paymaster, 130
McAram, W., 63
Maitland, Major-General Thomas, 66
Malcomb, Admiral Sir Pulteney, 166
Marie-Louise, Archduchess of Austria, 119
Marines, the (later Royal), 35
Marlborough, John Churchill, 1st Duke of, 10, 11, 13, 82
Marmont, Marshal Auguste, 125, 126
Marsac, Major Charles, 19, 190
Marsh, the Reverend William, 169
Martinique, 79, 82
Masséna, Marshal André, 119
Mediterranean Fleet, the, 63, 136
Melbourne, William Lamb, 2nd Viscount, 164, 165, 169
Melville, Henry Dundas, 1st Viscount, 66, 76
Mendip, Welbore Ellis, 1st Baron, 24, 148
Mendip, Lady (née Ann Stanley), 24, 148
Merton Hall, Norfolk, 22, (23)
Metternich, Prince, 145
Minorca, 63, 66
Miravete, Fort of, 115
Mirepoix, Maréchale de, 12
M'Kenzie, Captain, 113
Montfort, Henry Bromley, 1st Baron, 13, 14
Montego Bay, 98, (98)
Moore, Lieutenant-General Sir John, 98, 100
Morillo, General Pablo, 128
Mornington, Dowager, Countess, 74
Mornington, 1st Earl of, 71
Mornington, 3rd Earl of, 71, 119

Nancy, 11, 134
Naples, 60, 70, 82

Napoleon I, Emperor of France, 48, 59, 65, 72, 75, 79, 82, 87, 100, 119, 136, 141, 142, 144, 146
Navy, see Royal Navy
Nelson, Horatio, Vice-Admiral, Viscount, 8, 23, 26, 54, 59, 68, 69, 75, 79, 82, (83)
Nelson, Frances, Viscountess (née Woolard, formerly Nisbet), 23
Nelson, Memorial Commitee, the, 166
Nepean, Evan, 30
New Burlington Street, No. 3, 21, 24
Newfoundland, 30
Ney, Marshall Michel, 82, 119
Nichols, Major, 93
Nieman, River, 136
Nile, battle of the, 1798, 59
Nore, the, 55
North, Frederick, Lord, 17
North Sea Fleet, 136

Oldfield, Anne, (10), 11
Oporto, 98, 115
Orford, Horatio Walpole, 2nd Earl of, 12, 65, 98, 147
Orford, Horatio Walpole, 4th Earl of, 12, 14, 15, (19), 20
Orford, Horatio Walpole, 1st Earl of (N/C), 91
Orford, Sir Robert Walpole, 1st Earl of, 11, (11), (19)
Orford, Countess (née Skerret), 11, (11), (19)
Owen, Commodore (later Sir) Edward, 119

Pack, Lieutenant-Colonel Dennis, 94, 95
Paget, Lady Caroline, 150
Paget, Lady Charlotte, see Cadogan, Lady Charlotte
Paget, Sir Arthur, 105, 110, 135
Paget, Captain (later Sir) Charles, 87, 104, 110
Paget, Henry, Lord, see Anglesey, 1st Marquess of
Paget, William, 28
Paris, 25
Parker, Richard, 55
Pearce, Joseph, 17, 89, 91
Peel, Sir Robert, 150, 167, 169
Pellew, Captain Sir Edward, see Exmouth, 1st Baron
Pellew, Lady, 37
Pellew, Captain Israel, 55
Pennell, Michael, 63
Perceval, Spencer, 118, 136
Piccadilly, No. 138, 156
Pigot, Captain Hugh, 84, 85
Pitt, William (the Younger), 18, 19, 23, 26, 65, 82, 87
Plymouth, 7, 30, 37, 48, 53, 55, 59, 66, 68
Poland, 136
Popham, Captain (later Rear-Admiral) Sir Hume, 93
Portland, William Bentinck, 3rd Duke of, 18, 92, 118

Index

Index